County Down at War

1850–1945

Down Survey
2004

Yearbook of
Down County
Museum

Editor: Mike King

Published by
Down County Museum

County Down at War
1850–1945

Down Survey 2004
Yearbook of
Down County Museum

Editor: Mike King

Photography: G Allen Thompson

ISBN 0 9532530 7 4

Down Survey is a benefit of membership of the
Friends of Down County Museum. Membership
information is available from the museum at
  The Mall, Downpatrick,
  County Down BT30 6AH
  Telephone: 028 4461 5218
  Fax: 028 4461 5590
  Email: museum@downdc.gov.uk

Photographs:
Allen Thompson LBIPP: pages 9, 11, 12, 13, 14, 15, 17, 20,
21, 22, 23, 24, 33, 35, 37, 41, 42, 44, 47-50, 61, 85, 88-93,
99, 100, 103, 105, 107, 109
Ulster Museum: pages 43, 45
Ulster Folk and Transport Museum: page 87
Somme Heritage Centre Collection: pages 6, 26-32
North Down Heritage Centre Collection: pages 7, 95-97
Newry and Mourne Museum: page 18, 64
Kilmainham Gaol: pages 74-78
Down Recorder: page 4
Archives Service, Glasgow University: page 81
Michael Lee: page 71

Designed by Barry Craig

Printed by W&G Baird Ltd

Front cover illustration: Crayon drawing by William
Conor. Soldier at Newcastle Camp.
Badge, Spitfire Fund

Back cover: Sunset at Gallipoli, April 2004
(Courtesy of Brian Wilson)

Contents

Foreword

The year 2004 has seen some significant developments which I hope will benefit all those who enjoy visiting the Museum and contributing to its work of safeguarding and making accessible County Down's archaeology and history.

The first promising sign was the dramatic increase in the number of visitors attending the Museum, which rose from 38,901 in 2002-03 to 46,768 in 2003-04.

The second development was the very welcome support received from Down District Council and the Heritage Lottery Fund for the Governor's Residence Access Project. Costing just over £1.4m, this project will enable the Museum to make the Governor's Residence accessible to all, and install new displays telling the story of County Down over the last 10,000 years. The project has now commenced and the building will be open for St Patrick's Day 2006. The Council acknowledges the generous support of the Heritage Lottery Fund in enabling this project to go ahead in 2004.

The main temporary exhibition staged this year was entitled 'In Foreign Fields: the 13th Battalion of the Royal Irish Rifles in the Great War'. This exhibition was placed on loan to the Museum by the Somme Heritage Centre between 24th January and 1st July and was enhanced by displays of the Museum's own collections of items relating to the First World War.

The exhibition was supported by a book corner and a select booklist generously

Seascouts sitting on a First World War German gun outside the Old Gaol (Courtesy of the *Down Recorder*)

Photographs from a booklet sent by Colour Sergeant N Elphick of the 5th Battalion Royal Irish Rifles as a Christmas gift in 1911. Note the transformation of the raw recruit into the trained soldier on the steps of the Governor's Residence building (DCM 1989-27)

A group of Royal Engineers Signallers peeling potatoes in the courtyard of the Old Gaol, early in the First World War. On the left is Bob Grange, whose son Jack donated the photograph (Somme Heritage Centre collection)

researched and supplied by the SEELB and also by P6 pupils of Downpatrick Primary School who wrote some poignant poems to complement the display and summed up the reality of war in a few lines:

We Will Remember

Fighting in peril against the foe,
While watching some of their comrades fall.
Brave and young,
Marching with pride,
They face the foe.

So many a battle,
A tiresome fight.
The Flanders field,
Watched by larks
Who barely can be heard
Over cries of pain
And the bangs of guns.

A solemn home, such a common sight.
As families mourn,
They look at their short life,
memories.
They are sad but proud.

Hannah Lennon, age 11

The First and Second World Wars provide the main focus for the *Down Survey* 2004, entitled 'County Down at War'. Both the 90th anniversary of the beginning of the First World War and the 60th anniversary of D-Day were marked in 2004 and the commemorations created a natural focus for the current yearbook.

Over 20 articles have been assembled covering the period from the late nineteenth century to 1945. Particularly valuable contributions have been made by local people who have preserved special memories, artefacts and photographs of those who fought in the two World Wars. I am indebted to all the contributors, including teachers, specialists, editors, museum curators, archivists, council officers and local experts, for their scholarly accounts of the subject matter and for providing such a rich collection of photographs and illustrative material to bring the yearbook to life.

The articles have been deliberately selected to reveal key aspects of the wars and conflicts which touched County Down during this era, while ensuring that important collections and photographs are published and any interrelationships between the pieces

Veterans attending the unveiling of a Memorial Tablet to the 13th Battalion of the Royal Irish Rifles at Down Cathedral on 11 November 1928, by Col W Savage. The veterans are seen here assembled outside the Old Gaol on the Mall (Courtesy of North Down Heritage Collection)

highlighted. I am grateful to those contributors who have brought to my attention relevant photographs of the former County Gaol which I have used to illustrate this introduction.

The theme of the yearbook is particularly apt in the light of Down District Council's recent decision to begin work on a Book of Honour to commemorate those from the District who died during the two World Wars. Down County Museum will play an important role in creating the Book of Honour and we would like to receive any information from readers and relatives concerning individuals deserving of inclusion.

Finally, I would like to thank all those who have supported the Museum and its many projects during 2004, especially the Friends of the Museum for continuing to enhance the work of the Museum through their events, lectures and offers of financial assistance. I hope you enjoy reading the *Down Survey* and that perhaps one of the fascinating stories may spark an idea for a contribution of your own in a future edition.

Mike King
Museum Curator

Reflections on Commander Boatman George Colmer, HM Coastguard

Albert Colmer

George Colmer in his Coastguard uniform

The Coastguards of today are men and women, highly trained in marine search and rescue operations around the 4,500 mile coastline of the United Kingdom, who patrol many hundreds of miles far out into the Atlantic Ocean. The most up-to-date technology of the 21st century has meant its personnel are no longer desk-bound, spending long and tedious hours keeping watch, in lonely and remote lookout stations. Coastguard Officers now direct operations from specially equipped rescue centres, situated along the coastline. The majority of calls for help now reach the Coastguards through 999 emergency calls from the public or directly from vessels in the area using VHF radio.

The original Coastguard Service was set up in 1822, to crack down on smuggling and to stop the practice of deliberately wrecking ships, which entailed the luring of sailing ships on to the rocks, with the aid of flashing lights, so that their cargo could be salvaged from the sea, when the ships foundered. In those days smuggling was rife, with small fishing craft making landfall in narrow creeks and quiet harbours, with casks of brandy slung beneath their keels. Boats were found to have false bottoms and false bows, in which illegal liquor was hidden, and in some cases was stowed below their lobster creels.

The early Coastguards were expected to assist ships in distress, and in the case of shipwrecks, to do their utmost to save lives. Sadly, countless lives were lost, due to inability to get ashore from the stricken vessels; it was not until George Manby, a life-long friend of Horatio Nelson, developed a mortar which could fire a shot, with 500 yards of line attached, that shipwreck victims could be rescued by this means and brought to shore. Over the next 50 years many types of rockets were developed, and with the perfection of the 'Boxer Rocket' untold numbers of lives were saved between 1865 and 1946.

By the mid-1800s, the Coastguard Service had taken on a new role as a reserve force for the Navy, with some 3,000 Coastguards serving during the Crimean War; then the service passed from the Board of Customs to the Admiralty. The Coastguard Service Act came into force in 1856, giving the Coastguards the role of providing for the 'better defence of the coast of the Realm, and the more ready manning of the Navy'.

At this point I would like to introduce my grandfather, George Colmer. He was born on 13 November 1836, in the seaside village of St Germans, Cornwall. He joined the Navy at the age of 14 years 9 months, and he is described as having a 'fair complexion, hazel eyes and stature of 4 feet 11 inches'. His first ship was the *Impregnable*, which he joined as a Naval apprentice on 29 August 1851, transferring in quick succession to other ships, as was the custom of the time. He served on the *Penelope*,

HMS *Cambridge*

Coastguard cap badge worn
by George Colmer

Cornwallis, Haughty and the HMS *Cambridge*, which he joined on 18 May 1861.

Grandfather's next ship was the *Severn*, then he returned to the *Cambridge*, followed by the *Royal George* in 1867, the *Pallas, Audacious, Vanguard* and the *Iron Duke* in 1875. (The HMS *Cambridge* was launched in 1755, and she is recorded as still being in service in the late 1890s, when she was being used as a floating gunnery school).

My grandfather, whilst serving on the *Penelope* in 1854 and the *Cornwallis* in 1855, received the 'Baltic Medal'. He also served during the First Opium War and the Anglo-Chinese War. On 1 June 1857, when on the gunboat *Haughty*, a number of gunboats, including his, were sent to attack a group of Chinese pirate junks hidden in Escape Creek and Fatshan Creek on the Canton River. Gunboats were ideal for this job. They were steam-powered, carried one main gun capable of long range firing, and were specifically designed to operate in shallow waters like those of the Canton River. The fleet of junks was destroyed. He was awarded the China Medal with two Bars – Fatshan 1857 and Canton 1857. In 1860 he was awarded a third Bar for an attack on Taku Forts, and in 1870 he was awarded the Medal 'For Long

Service and Good Conduct', inscribed along its edge 'Geo Colmer Comd Boatmn H M Coast Gd'.

Somehow my grandfather found time to 'win the hand' of Charlotte McClinchey, from Killough, Co Down, daughter of Hugh McClinchey, Master Baker. They were married in Rathmullan Parish Church on 17 June 1868, and from the union they had four children, Robert, George, Emma and Albert, my father.

Grandfather was posted to Ireland in 1880. Arriving in Tramore, Co Waterford, he and his wife and family moved into the Coastguard Station, which is now the Garda Siochana Police HQ for the area. From there he was posted to Cushendall, Co Antrim, then to Annalong, Co Down, and eventually to the Coastguard Station in Killough, as Officer in Charge.

The original Coastguard Station at Killough was located near to St John's Point Light House, but it was closed down in 1845, and moved to Killough, near to the harbour. The present terraced Coastguard Station was built in about 1870, a fortified building with gun loops, due to the Government's fear at the time of possible attack from the Fenians, who were active in the 1860 Rebellion. My grandfather died in office, on 25

George and Charlotte Colmer pictured with two of their four children

March 1893 at the age of 56, and his widow and children had to vacate their home in the Coastguard Station, which was standard procedure. He was buried in the graveyard of Killough Parish Church.

Grandfather's three sons all developed professions associated with the sea. My father served his apprenticeship with Harland and Wolff as an engine fitter, travelling to South Africa to work in East London, and coming back to work on the ill-fated *Titanic*. He was due to sail on her maiden voyage, but at the last moment he left the ship due to a premonition that something was wrong, but that is a story for another time...

My father served with the Coastguards during World War Two, and for some time after that,

George Colmer's gravestone in the graveyard of Killough Parish Church

Albert Colmer senior, in uniform, pictured in Coney Island, in 1944 (All photographs courtesy of Albert Colmer)

Albert Colmer pictured with his grandfather's sword and telescope, October 2004 (Down County Museum)

being recommended for his service medal, and I became a member of the Auxiliary Coastguard, reg no ARD 39, in 1979. To mark the service of three generations of the Colmer family in the Coastguards, the original uniform worn by George Colmer was lent for display in Down County Museum's *Sea of Life* exhibition in 2003. His sword, telescope and medals have also survived and remain proud family possessions; George himself would have had a wonderful story to tell, if only he was present to tell it.

Albert Colmer is the founder member of the Lecale Historical Society, and was editor for 20 years of its journal the Lecale Miscellany. He has been a Down District Councillor for 16 years and was Chairman in the year 2000.

Albert Colmer's membership card of the Auxiliary Coastguard Service

The South Down Militia and the Boer War, 1901–2

Marcus Crichton

In September 2002 Down County Museum staged a small exhibition in the Governor's Residence building, commemorating those local men who fought in the Boer War. A number of artefacts and photographs from the Museum's collection were put on display, together with several loans from the Royal Irish Rifles Museum in Belfast. The display included old photographs, gallantry medals won by individuals, and equipment used by the soldiers, such as a pith helmet, bayonets and a standard issue British Army rifle of the period.

The exhibition also acted as a prelude to a new play, *Soldiers of the Queen*, by Damien Smyth, which was performed in the Down Arts Centre on 2-5 October 2002. Set in South Africa at the height of the Boer War, the play provided a vivid portrayal of the experiences of a Downpatrick soldier fighting in a distant land.

Both the exhibition and play were prompted by the centenary of the return home of County Down soldiers, after spending a year of active service in South Africa, fighting in the Boer War.

The 5th Battalion Royal Irish Rifles, better known as the South Down Militia, was based in Downpatrick and comprised largely men from South Down. However, the County Down countryside was soon to become a distant memory when the soldiers, under their commanding officer, Colonel R H Wallace of Myra Castle, near Strangford, sailed from Queenstown, now Dunlaoghaire, on Good Friday, 5 April 1901, to take up arms in South Africa.

When they returned to Queenstown just over a year later on 28 June 1902 their numbers had been significantly reduced. In all, 31 men of the 5th Battalion, including one officer, met their deaths in the bloody conflict, which was the first major war of the twentieth century. A commemorative plaque in Down Cathedral bears their names, and those of two riflemen of the 4th Battalion of the Royal Irish Rifles, who also lost their lives.

A small paragraph in the *Down Recorder* of 6 April 1901, announced the departure of the South Down Militia:

Colonel Wallace, commanding officer of the South Downs, pictured in South Africa during the Boer War

In Memory of
COLOR SERGT CHAS LEATHEM,
5TH BN ROYAL IRISH RIFLES.
(ROYAL SOUTH DOWNS)
WHO DIED AT KROONSTAD,
8TH FEBRUARY 1902.

ERECTED BY HIS COMRADES.

The grave of
Colour Sergeant
Charles Leathem,
who died at
Kroonstad, 8
February 1902

The 5th Royal Irish Rifles, to the number of 25 officers and 671 non-commissioned officers and men, left Enniskillen by special train at midnight on Thursday for Queenstown, where they embarked on the Wakool yesterday for South Africa. The officers are Colonel R H Wallace, commanding; Majors W G Forde and J M Morrison; Captains C H Edye, G E H Barrett-Hamilton, W M Cole-Hamilton, G A Chatterton, B C James and F A Stokes.

Lt Seeds was soon to be promoted to captain, but he did not live long to enjoy his new rank, succumbing to dysentery within two months of disembarking in South Africa. He was the only officer of the South Downs to die in the war.

Colonel Wallace was an able and popular commanding officer. He joined the South Downs in 1879 and was to have a connection with the regiment lasting 34 years. When the Boer War broke out in 1899, Wallace sent postcards to all his battalion, asking the officers and men if they were willing to volunteer for service at the front. There was a unanimous response. Consequently, the battalion was embodied at Downpatrick on 10 May 1900, and proceeded to Enniskillen and Derry. Having volunteered three times for active service, the offer was finally accepted and the South Downs sailed for South Africa, arriving in Cape Town on 28 April 1901.

They were assigned the task of protecting the railway line between Cape Town and Pretoria, and within a month had sustained their first

Memorial plaque in Down Cathedral to the men of the Royal South Down Militia, who lost their lives in the Boer War

casualties in battle. Private M Rooney, 'B' company, and Lance Corporal J Mahood, 'F' company, were both killed in action on 17 May and were described by Col Wallace as 'good and gallant soldiers.'

More were to die in the 12 months of combat to follow as the South Downs distinguished themselves in combat and established a reputation as fearless fighters. When the Boers finally surrendered in June 1902, the South Downs were among the first British detachments to receive surrendering Boer commandos.

Later that month when they were ordered to leave their position, the South Downs were given 'a hearty send-off' by their former enemies.

The esteem in which they were held by their fellow soldiers is evident in the following order issued by a senior British officer, Major-General Sir W G Knox: 'On the departure of the 5th Battalion the GOC begs to testify to the loyal support which at all times he has received from Colonel Wallace and the other ranks of this fine unit during their stay in South Africa.'

Marcus Crichton is deputy editor of the *Down Recorder*.

Samuel Craig, a Young Soldier in the Great War

Samuel Craig

Samuel Craig, my father, was only 17 when he enlisted in the 9th Battalion of the Royal Irish Rifles in Downpatrick on 29 April 1915, along with his friend Connelly Pepper. Born in 1897 and living in Scotch Street, Downpatrick, he was one of the many teenagers who flocked to the recruiting stations in County Down in late 1914 and early 1915.

After basic training at Ballykinlar Camp, Samuel was transferred to Sussex-on-Sea and from there to France. By this time he had been promoted to Lance Sergeant, in charge of a Lewis machine gun corps. The photograph taken of Samuel after the war in 1919 shows his Sergeant stripes on his right arm with the 'LG' (Lewis Gunner) badge above, and his four stripes for four years service below.

Samuel was one of only a handful of the 9th who came back from the Battle of the Somme on 1 July 1916. As he recalled, when interviewed on the seventieth anniversary of the battle in 1986:"I was one of 87 survivors in our battalion. After that they combined us with the 12th". The Battle of the Somme had all but wiped out the 9th Battalion.

Sergeant Samuel Craig, pictured after the Great War in 1919

Samuel Craig's medals from the Great War

Samuel Craig pictured as a prisoner-of-war in 1918

Sgt. Samuel. Craig
12" Irish Rifles

1918.

The Queen joins me in welcoming you on your release from the miseries & hardships, which you have endured with so much patience & courage.

During these many months of trial, the early rescue of our gallant Officers & Men from the cruelties of their captivity has been uppermost in our thoughts.

We are thankful that this longed for day has arrived, & that back in the old Country you will be able once more to enjoy the happiness of a home & to see good days among those who anxiously look for your return.

George R.I.

Letter of George V to Samuel Craig welcoming him home from his captivity as a prisoner-of-war in 1918

Serial No. 24365   Records XI District

Army Form Z. 21.

CERTIFICATE of* { Discharge / Transfer to Reserve / Disembodiment / Demobilization } on Demobilization.

Regtl. No. 458 ... Rank Lance Sergeant

Names in full Craig Samuel
(Surname first)

Unit and Regiment or Corps from which
*Discharged
Transferred to Reserve
Enlisted on the ...... 29 April ....191 5.

For Roy...... ......
(Here state Regiment for Corps to which first appointed)

Also served in...

....

Only Regiments or Corps in which the Soldier served since August 4th, 1914, are to be stated. If inapplicable, this space is to be ruled through in ink and initialled.

†Medals and Decorations awarded during present engagement
*Has / Has not served Overseas on Active Service.

Authorized prior to 11 11 18

Place of Rejoining in case of emergency Belfast   Medical Category: A I

Specialist Military qualifications nil   Year of birth 1897

He is* { Discharged / Transferred to Army Reserve / Disembodied / Demobilized } Class Z on 24 March 1919 in consequence of Demobilization.

............................Signature and Rank.

Officer i/c .... Records. ....(Place).

* Strike out whichever is inapplicable.   † The word "Nil" to be inserted when necessary.

(20998). Wt. W 8211—P.P. 2329. 3,000m. 1/19. D & S. (E 1256.)

WARNING.—If this Certificate is lost, a duplicate cannot be issued. You should therefore on no account part with it or forward it by post when applying for a situation.

N.B.—Any person finding this Certificate is requested to forward it, in an unstamped envelope, to the Secretary, War Office, London, S.W.1.

Samuel Craig's Certificate of Transfer to the Reserve, issued on 24 March 1919, recording his award of the Military Medal (All photographs courtesy of Samuel Craig).

Later in the war, Samuel was awarded the Military Medal for bravery in manning a machine gun post under heavy fire at the battle of Messines in June 1917. His highly prized medals, still in my possession, also include the 1914–15 Star, the British War Medal and the British Victory Medal.

However, Samuel did not finish the war on the battlefield, as he was captured by the Germans and made a prisoner-of-war at St Quintin in March 1918. As he recalled seventy years later: "I spent the last nine months of the war as a prisoner-of-war but I cannot complain about the way I was treated".

On his release in November 1918, Samuel received a letter from King George V, welcoming him home from his captivity. He was released along with his old friend, Connelly Pepper, who had enlisted in Downpatrick on the same day as my father, three and a half years earlier.

Samuel Craig joined the RAF in 1940 and served as a rear gunner in 67 missions in Wellington bombers in the North African and Italian campaigns, before becoming a commissioned air gunner instructor at RAF Manby, and serving in gunnery schools in Dumfries, Morpeth and Bishopscourt from July 1943. He earned six medals and the rank of Flight Lieutenant when he left Bishopscourt for demobilisation in August 1946.

An Anti-Conscription Election Poster of 1918

Noreen Cunningham

In the archive collections of Newry and Mourne Museum is an enigmatic document which on first examination seems to be a First World War anti-conscription poster. Research however has shown that this poster alludes to another 'battle' that had already commenced for the hearts and minds of the Irish Nationalist electorate.

The poster leads with the title 'Who are They who want to help the English Government to Conscript You?' followed by a list of Parliamentarians who, on 'the 17th of January, last, in the English House of Commons would not vote against Conscription for Ireland'. The poster ends with the exhortation to 'Vote for McCartan and Down with the Consc[r]iptionists'.

Conscription was the compulsory enlistment of men for active service in the First World War, and various levels of conscription were introduced in a series of Military Service Acts from 1916 onwards. These acts were precipitated by a fall in recruitment from 1915 onwards right across the British Isles, possibly due to heavy losses sustained on the Western Front, and growing apathy at home. Anti-English sentiment generated after the events of the 1916 Easter Rising may not have been such an important factor to account for the fall in Irish enlistment as previously thought[1]; nevertheless the threat of conscription became a contentious issue in Irish politics after 1916.

One of the parliamentarians listed who 'would

Who are They who want to help the English Government to Conscript You?

HERE THEY ARE!

This is a List of the Parliamentarians who on the 17th of January, last, in the English House of Commons, would not Vote against Conscription for Ireland:—

Boyle, Daniel, North Mayo
Byrne, A., Dublin Harbour
Clancy, J. J., Dublin, North
Cosgrove, James, Galway East
Crumley, P., Fermanagh South
Devlin, Joseph, Belfast West
Dillon, John, Mayo West
Donelan, Captain, Wicklow East
Donovan, J. T., Wicklow West
Doris, W , Mayo West
Duffy, W. J., Galway South
Esmonde, Captain, Tipperary North
Esmonde, Sir Thomas, Wexford North
Farrell, J. P., Longford North
French, P., Wexford South
Field, William, Dublin St. Patrick's
Fitzpatrick, J. C., Ossory.
Fitzgibbon, John, Mayo South
Flavin, M., Kerry North
Gwynn, Stephen, Galway South
Hackett, J., Tipperary Mid.
Hazleton, Richard, Galway North
Hearn, Michael, Dublin South
Joyce, Alderman, Limerick City
Kelly, E., Donegal East
Kennedy, Vincent, Cavan West
Kilbride, A., Kildare South
Lundon, Thomas, Limerick East

McGhee, Richard, Tyrone Mid.-
MacNeill, Swift, Donegal South
Meagher, Michael, Kilkenny North
Meehan, Francis, Leitrim North
Meehan, P. J., Leix
Molloy, M., Carlow
Mooney, John J., Newry
Muldoon, John, Cork East
Murphy, M. J., Waterford East
Nolan, Joseph, Louth South
Nugent, J. D., Dublin College Green
Nugent, Sir Walter, Westmeath, South
O'Connor, T. P., Liverpool
O'Doherty, Philip,- Donegal North
O'Donnell, Thomas,- Kerry West
O'Dowd, John, Sligo South
O'Shaughnessy, P. J., Limerick West
O'Shee, J. J., Waterford West
O'Sullivan, T., Kerry East
Reddy, Michael, Birr
Redmond, J. E., Waterford
Redmond, W. A., Tyrone East
Sheehy, David, Meath South
Smyth, T. P., Leitrim South
White, Patrick, Meath North
Whitty, P. J., Louth North
Young, Samuel, Cavan East

Vote for McCARTAN and Down with the Consciptionists.

Anti-conscription election poster of January 1918 (Courtesy of Newry and Mourne Museum: NMM: 2004:14)

not vote against conscription' being extended to Ireland is Newry MP, John Joseph Mooney. But in a sense Newry had already been wiped off the electoral map. In 1917 alterations to the electoral constituencies meant that Newry was no longer a separate parliamentary borough, but was submerged within the constituency of South Down. This was a great blow to civic pride, and Newry, for the first time since this privilege was granted in a Charter of James I in 1613, was unable to return a parliamentary candidate.[2]

What the poster actually refers to is a by-election contest that was precipitated by the death of the MP for Armagh South, Dr Charles O'Neill, who was a member of the Irish Parliamentary Party (IPP). Formed in 1882 under the leadership of Charles Stewart Parnell and others, the IPP was instrumental in laying the groundwork for Irish self-government. In the years after 1916 however, the IPP was increasingly being challenged at the polls by Sinn Féin, who had moved away from being an Irish separatist monarchist party to campaigning in 1917 for an Irish Republic. Due to the First World War, no election had taken place between 1910 and 1918, and each by-election that arose was a fiercely contested fight between the two parties. Despite being staunchly IPP, Armagh South was seen as an important testing ground for Sinn Féin, who despite winning a number of by-elections in the south of the country, had not mirrored this success in the north.

A pressing problem for Sinn Féin was finding a suitable nominee to run for election. In the absence of a local candidate, Dr Patrick McCartan[3] from Carrickmore in Tyrone was put forward, much to his own surprise, after reading his nomination in a New York newspaper.[4] McCartan was not present for the election campaign; he was Sinn Féin envoy in the United States and worked in a New York hospital. The IPP selected a good local candidate, Patrick Donnelly, who was a well-known Newry solicitor. Both parties fought the election in a very planned way, with Sinn Féin organising it as a military operation, drafting in volunteers from as far away as Cork, Kerry and Clare.[5] Fights between the IPP and Sinn Féin broke out on a number of occasions in towns throughout the area and there was also heckling and confrontation between the two parties in Newry. Although outside the constituency, Newry saw a lot of electioneering, with Sinn Féin winding up its campaign on 31 January with a rally in Margaret Square, attended by senior party figures including Eamon de Valera, Countess Markievicz and Arthur Griffith.[6]

At the polls, on 2 February 1918, the IPP outstripped Sinn Féin, with Donnelly getting 2,324 and McCartan 1,305 votes. Although Sinn Féin did not win this by-election, they saw a huge increase in support that was later reflected in the December 1918 election.[7]

In conclusion, rather than simply being an anti-conscription poster, this document is evidence of one of the many sorties that was to take place between the Irish Parliamentary Party and Sinn Féin in the run-up to the general election of December 1918. Many historians see this election as a key defining moment in modern Irish history. It saw the decimation of The Irish Parliamentary Party and the emergence of Sinn Féin as a dominant electoral force.

Noreen Cunningham is Curator of Newry and Mourne Museum and is involved in a Heritage Lottery Fund project which will see the relocation of the museum to Bagenal's Castle in Newry. Prior to working in the museum sector, Noreen worked for many years as an archaeologist. She has an Honours degree in Archaeology and Social Anthropology and a Masters in Cultural Management.

Notes and References
1. Jeffrey, K, *Ireland and the Great War*, (2000), pp 6-10.
2. Canavan, T, *Frontier Town, An Illustrated History of Newry*, (1989), p 182.
3. Dr Patrick McCartan, F.R.C.S.I., 10 Fitzwilliam Square Dublin. Member of the Sinn Féin Party; Dublin Corporation, 1908-9; Member of the National Council Sinn Féin, 1905-7; Editor "Irish Freedom," 1905–11; Dublin Correspondent of the "Gaelic American," 1905–11; Envoy to America, 1917-20; Envoy to Moscow, 1920–21; MP and TD for North Offaly, 1918-23. (*Seanad Éireann*, Volume 4, 5 March 1925).
4. Feeney, B, *Sinn Féin, A Hundred Turbulent Years*, (2002), p 86.
5. Feeney, B, *Sinn Féin, A Hundred Turbulent Years*, (2002), p 87.
6. Watson, Raymond P, *Cath Saoirse An Iúir; Newry's Struggle*.
7. The result of this election was Sinn Féin 73 seats, Unionists 26 seats and Nationalists 6 seats.

The Peake Brothers at War, 1914–1918

Harold Gordon

When I heard that Down County Museum was mounting an exhibition about the County Down men who served in the First World War, 90 years after the outbreak of that terrible conflict in 1914, I took the opportunity to share with museum staff the story of my three uncles, William John Peake (known as Jack), Reuben Herbert Peake and Joseph Hadden Peake, who all joined up in Newtownards, County Down.

My uncles were the sons of John and Elizabeth Peake. John came from Glasgow to Downpatrick in the 1880s and eventually settled on the estate of Lord Dunleath at Ballywalter. John was a cabinet maker and French polisher, and survived to the grand old age of 93. He died on 25 June 1954 and was buried in Whitechurch Cemetery, Ballywalter. John and Elizabeth had 8 children: Jack was the oldest, born in 1892, then came Dora, Mabel (my mother), Reuben and then Eddie, who died young. Next came Joe and Bobbie, who were twins, born on 11 January 1900 at the very beginning of the new century, and finally Kathleen arrived in 1904.

When the First World War began, Jack was old enough to join up. He joined the 13th Battalion, 36th Ulster Division of the Royal Irish Rifles, becoming a Corporal. Reuben, only 17, grew a moustache and succeeded in joining the 7th Battalion of the Royal Irish Rifles. Jack arrived in France in October 1915, and on 8 December he sent a Christmas card, which still survives, to his sister Mabel.[1] After basic battle training, his unit

Christmas card from Jack Peake to his sister Mabel, 8 Dec 1915 (Courtesy of Harold Gordon)

Jack Peake's First World War medals (Courtesy of Harold Gordon)

Reuben Peake (right) and two soldiers of the Leinster Regiment in a military hospital, 1917 (Courtesy of Harold Gordon)

headed for the Somme area, where it sheltered in the Avelvy Wood. On the fateful 1 July, the opening day of the battle of the Somme, Jack was called into action. The battle commenced at 7.30am along a 20-mile front. Jack distinguished himself by leading his men over the top after his sergeant was killed, and for that he earned the Military Medal. He was killed in action that same day, aged 24, and he was buried at Thiepval. Two of his friends from Ballywalter, Edward Curry and Robert Regan, died alongside him. His highly prized medals were passed on to me by my aunt Kathleen, who died in 1985.

Rifleman Reuben Peake was wounded in action on the Western Front, and spent some time convalescing in a hospital in England before returning home for a short time in 1917. A surviving photograph of him, with two fellow soldiers from the Leinster Regiment, was probably taken at the hospital where he was treated. He later returned to Flanders and fought in the Third Battle of Ypres. He was killed near Ypres on Wednesday 8 August 1917, when the military hospital where he was lying wounded was bombed by the enemy. His name is inscribed on the Menin Gate, Ypres, with a total of 55,000 names of those lost or killed in action. The Menin Gate is one of four memorials to the missing in Belgian Flanders, which cover the area known as the Ypres Salient. Reuben's and Jack's names are also inscribed on the War

The Menin Gate,
Ypres

Joe Peake in the
uniform of the
Royal Engineers
(Courtesy of
Harold Gordon)

The Peake family home at 38 Church Street, Downpatrick (Courtesy of Nina Gregory)

Postcard from William Gregory to his wife, showing his regiment training on Salisbury Plain, September 1904 (Courtesy of Nina Gregory)

Memorial monument in their home village of Ballywalter.

The third brother, Joe Peake, although under age, joined the Royal Engineers, fully stretching his joinery skills in the construction of all the things needed to service the war. Joe's love of horses was another asset in the First World War, as he helped to look after and prepare horses before they were shipped to Cherbourg, France. A photograph of Joe in uniform survives in our family archive. After Jack and Reuben had been killed, Lord Dunleath made a special request that Joe was not sent to France. As a result, he survived the war, and followed in his father's footsteps to become an accomplished carpenter. His skill with wood can be seen in his restoration work in Balligan Church, where the pews, panelling and pulpit were all his work. Joe continued to work on the Dunleath estate until his retirement, and lived to the grand old age of 91.

The Peake family was related by marriage to William Gregory (known as Willie), who married Sarah, sister of Elizabeth Peake, on 17 December 1902.

William and Sarah lived with John Peake's unmarried brother, William Peake, at 38 Church Street, Downpatrick, where the latter ran a grocery and confectionery shop. William Gregory was a schoolteacher by profession, and a keen cricketer. Willie joined the army long before the First World War, and served in the Royal Artillery. A postcard sent to his wife at 38 Church Street on 30 September 1904, shows his regiment training in southern England, with a mark made above Willie's head in the ranks. A surviving photograph shows that he played in a regimental cricket team while away in the army.

At the outbreak of the First World War, Willie was transferred to France to man the heavy Howitzer guns, which were used to bombard

William Gregory in a regimental cricket team, middle row, second from left (Courtesy of Nina Gregory)

William Gregory pictured with Downpatrick Cricket Team, c 1930, front row, 4th from left (Courtesy of Nina Gregory)

the enemy. Despite suffering from shell shock, Willie survived the war and returned home to Downpatrick, where he got a job in the Motor Taxation Office. He became a well-known figure in Downpatrick, especially on the cricket field, where he played and later umpired with distinction.

The family's military service continued in the Second World War, when William and Sarah's son, Ted, joined the army.[2] Ted's wife, Florence (known as Florie) joined the ATS and worked for most of the War in Ballykinlar Camp. My brother, Reuben, joined the Home Guard in 1940, at times manning an anti-aircraft gun stationed where the Parish Church of St Ignatius stands today at Carryduff, on the Comber Road. This was one of the few guns which protected Belfast against air raids during 1941–2.

When I remember the ultimate sacrifice made by my uncles, Jack and Reuben, in the First World War, I recall how in his later years my uncle Joe often recalled his brothers and those legions of friends gone before. The familiar words said in tribute at Joe's funeral were particularly poignant:

> They shall grow not old as we that are left grow old – age shall not weary them nor the years condemn, at the going down of the sun and in the morning we will remember them. And Joe did.

Harold Gordon is a life-long supporter of the British Legion and has been a poppy seller for Remembrance Day since 1993.

Notes
1. My mother, Mabel, worked for Lord Dunleath as an assistant cook in her early teens, and during the First World War she volunteered as an auxiliary nurse, looking after injured Belgian soldiers on Lord Dunleath's estate at Ballywalter.
2. Ted's sister, Lorna, will be remembered as the deputy organist at Down Cathedral, and a dedicated piano teacher in Downpatrick.

The 13th Battalion (1st County Down Volunteers) The Royal Irish Rifles in the First World War

Craig McGuicken

During the First World War it is estimated that more than 210,000 Irishmen served in the British forces. Thousands more would fight in the armies of Australia, New Zealand and the USA. An unknown number of Irishwomen – certainly several thousand – would also do their bit for the war effort.

Men from all over Ireland and from all kinds of backgrounds joined up. Around 30,000 members of the Ulster Volunteers and a similar number from the Irish Volunteers enlisted. By 1918 these old enemies would have fought side by side on a number of occasions. The hardships of the trenches, like German bullets, did not differentiate between rich or poor, Catholic or Protestant. It is estimated that more than 30,000 Irish died in 'The Great War'.

The purpose of this article is to focus on just one unit – the 13th Battalion of the Royal Irish Rifles (13th RIR), who were largely raised from County Down.

Herbert McCready of Bangor. McCready rose to the rank of Regimental Sergeant-Major with the 13th RIR. He was wounded at the Somme and taken prisoner, but survived the war. He died in 1962. His 'Down' shoulder title is clearly visible (Somme Heritage Centre Collection)

Down Goes to War

The story of the 13th RIR begins in the Home Rule Crisis which was the dominant political issue in Irish and British politics in the years immediately prior to the First World War. The 'Unionists' of Ulster, distrustful of both the British Government and the Nationalist population of Ireland, responded to the threat of Home Rule by forming the Ulster Volunteers (UVF).

The UVF began training and drilling on an informal basis, but soon became centrally organised along the Territorial Army structure. Local units were formed all over Ulster, and were divided into regiments, battalions, companies, sections and even squads. By the end of 1913 the UVF numbered 90,000. It included a special service force (guarding Headquarters staff), an intelligence unit, a motor car and motor cycle section, signalling and nursing corps. In response, Nationalists formed the Irish Volunteers. The prospect of civil war loomed large over Ireland.

Local hostilities ceased however, with the outbreak of European war in August 1914. Edward Carson and John Redmond, the respective leaders of Ulster Unionism and Irish Nationalism, offered their forces to the British Army. Down was at war.

Forming the Down Battalion

To meet the demands of an expanded army, the existing Irish regiments formed new battalions. The RIR traditionally recruited in Counties Antrim and Down, and the city of Belfast. Many of the recruits from County Down were members of local units of the UVF. Often, local officers would arrive at the training camp or recruiting office with a group of volunteers who would join up en masse. Recruits from Down, usually became members of the 13th RIR.

The main training camp for the 13th RIR was at Clandeboye, between Bangor and

Members of North Down Volunteers in 1914. These men possibly all worked in Andrews Mill in Comber. Frequently groups of friends, or workmates would join up together. Often local landowners and industrialists would encourage men to enlist, and would even form local units (Somme Heritage Centre Collection)

Newtownards. From 15 to 24 September, 27 officers and 1143 'other ranks' joined the Battalion, making it the largest in the 'Ulster Division'. Colonel W H Savage was appointed Battalion Commander, and the majority of his officers were ex-UVF. The men were formed into four Companies:

'A' – men from Holywood, Bangor, Donaghadee and Ards districts

'B' – Ballygowan, Comber, Newtownards and Ards

'C' – Killyleagh, Downpatrick, Ballynahinch, Dromore, Hillsborough, Castlewellan and Newcastle

'D' – Banbridge, Rathfriland, Gilford, Kilkeel and Newry

Volunteer to Soldier

Training was in full swing by the end of September 1914. Initially training consisted of drill and route marches of up to 25 miles. Later, more varied field exercises and more specific training was provided – trench warfare, night attacks, unit manoeuvres and musketry. The men received lessons in French, and officers were sent on specialist courses. Lack of equipment was a problem during this period. Frequently, rifle training was done with old UVF weapons. The officers 'made do' by replacing the relevant military equipment with objects of similar size and weight. For example, shipyard bolts were used in place of ammunition in belts and backpacks could be weighed down with stones.

During this period the Battalion suffered its first casualty. William J Prichard from Greyabbey died from pneumonia on 26 October 1914, in Holywood Hospital.

On 8 May 1915, Major General Sir Hugh McCalmont inspected the entire Ulster Division at Malone. Afterwards they paraded through the streets of Belfast. The band of the 13th played 'The Mountains of Mourne'. Two months later, the Ulster Division moved to Seaford on the Sussex coast, to complete their training. On 30 September 1915, King George V reviewed the Division and a few days later they sailed for France.

The Military Haircut, Clandeboye Camp, 1914. This photograph was taken before training had begun in earnest. One advantage that the Irish recruiting authorities had was that many recruits had some basic military training due to membership of the Ulster or Irish Volunteers (Courtesy of Mr L Morrow)

The Band of the 13th RIR. The band was important for the unit's confidence and its sense of identity. The strong territorial basis on which the Ulster Division had been raised was important in creating a sense of purpose and duty (Courtesy of Mr L Morrow)

To France

The 13th Rifles arrived in France in early October 1915. To help new units adjust to the conditions, they were attached to more experienced ones. Therefore, the men of the 13th accompanied the Warwickshire Regiment into the trenches for the first time on 19 October. Three days later Rifleman Thomas Quinn became the Battalion's first casualty (wounded) of enemy action.

During this period the Ulstermen underwent 'battle-hardening', to prepare them for combat, and were slowly acclimatised to the new conditions. They also assisted in preparations for the 'big push', as the offensive planned by General Haig was known. They converted barns into troop accommodation, constructed horse lines and even helped lay a railway for the transport of stores and ammunition. They also spent time cleaning streets and repairing buildings in the villages of the Somme region.

In February 1916, the Ulster Division was finally given a sector of the line to hold in the Mesnil area. The 13th worked closely with the 11th RIR, rotating between reserve and the front-line. By June, the Division's operational area had

Leaving Clandeboye for England, July 1915. This picture shows the men marching from Clandeboye to the train station in Newtownards. From there they travelled to Dublin, then to Holyhead, and finally to Seaford in East Sussex (Somme Heritage Centre Collection)

Members of 'C' Company in Reserve, near Auchonvillers. This picture shows how the soldiers tried to combat the conditions in France. They are wearing sheepskins which helped to keep them warm, but also kept warm some uninvited guests – lice. On their legs they are wearing a type of 'wader' developed for the trenches, which helped prevent trench-foot (Courtesy of Mr L Morrow)

An unknown soldier of the 13th RIR, in 'Bond Street' Trench. This photograph was taken near Auchonvillers in the Somme area, in the winter of 1915–16 (Courtesy of Mr L Morrow)

shifted southward. The 13th were now located around a previously quiet area near the River Ancre – Thiepval Wood.

Between landing in France in October 1915 and the eve of the Somme on 1 July 1916, the Battalion had suffered 153 casualties, including 44 dead.

The Somme

The Battle of the Somme was the first major action for many of the men of Kitchener's 'new armies', and involved both the 16th (Irish) and 36th (Ulster) Divisions. The British had decided on an attack in the Somme area after consultation with their French allies, who were under enormous pressure in Verdun. The 'big push' would break the stalemate on the Western Front.

The attack was launched at 7.30am on 1 July 1916. Along a twenty-mile front more than 200,000 British and French troops attacked strongly-held German positions. A massive artillery barrage, which had begun on 24 June, should have destroyed the German defences and allowed the troops to make a swift advance through the enemy lines.

The Ulster Division attacked from Thiepval Wood, along the River Ancre, and towards the village of Grandcourt. Initially they made good progress, reaching all of their objectives. However, as the day wore on, the Ulstermen began to suffer from high casualty rates, and a lack of water and ammunition. Large numbers of German reserves, allied to a lack of support troops, forced them to fall back to the German 'A' lines.

By the time the Ulster Division was removed from the line on 3 July, it had suffered more than 5,000 casualties, including over 2,000 dead. The Commanding Officer of the 13th summed up the chaos and carnage of 1 July in his diary entry for 7.30 am of that morning – 'From this time I received no messages, the Companies were lost'. Of the 800 men of the 13th RIR who entered the trenches on 1 July, only 182 would walk out the following day. Of the rest, more than 200 were dead.

The Destruction of the 13th

By mid July 1916, the remnants of the 13th had moved to Belgium. Due to losses at the Somme they were temporarily amalgamated with the 11th RIR – until both units received the necessary reinforcements.

The Ulster Division was involved in two major actions in Belgium in 1917. The success of the first led to the disaster of the second. On 7 June 1917 the Ulstermen, fighting side by side with the

German prisoners of the Ulster Division, 1 July 1916. The Ulster Division captured over 500 German prisoners (Courtesy of Mr L Morrow)

men of the 16th (Irish) Division, attacked the German positions on the Messines Ridge. Although the 13th were in reserve for the actual attack, they moved forward that evening to consolidate the gains. Meticulously planned by General Plumer, the attack was the greatest British success of the War so far.

Encouraged, the British pressed on with a series of offensives which have become known simply as 'Passchandaele'. On 16 August the Division, including the 13th, attacked the German positions around Langemarck. The assault got bogged down in the Flanders mud, as the men came under intense fire from German defenders in concrete 'pill boxes'.

When the 13th Rifles left the line on 18 August, they were battered and exhausted. Belgian mud, German bullets and British tactics had devastated the Division.

To the End

The 13th moved south in November 1917 and was amalgamated with the 11th Rifles. By now recruits were becoming harder to find and gradually the old 'Down' identity of the Battalion was disappearing.

The Battle of Cambrai began in November 1917, just south of the old Somme battlefields. The initial British attacks, led by large numbers of tanks, were very successful. However, by the time the 13th entered the fray the impetus had been lost. By December the men were fighting under some of the worst conditions they had experienced, and by the end of the month most of the British gains had been lost.

By February 1918, it had been decided that the losses of some units were no longer sustainable, particularly as the British army was now required to hold a longer front. The 11th/13th RIR were disbanded, and most of the remnants joined the

H A Uprichard of Tullylish, Gilford, Commanding Officer of 'D' Coy. Uprichard died on 1 July, and is buried at Mill Road Cemetery, Thiepval (Courtesy of Mr L Morrow)

Rifleman John McCance of Dundrum. McCance was born in Dundrum, enlisted in Downpatrick and died at Passchandaele. He has no known grave and is commemorated on the Tyne Cot memorial, along with 35,000 others. Before the battle had even begun, the Ulster Division had suffered over 2000 casualties, rising to 3,500 by the time of their removal from the line (Courtesy of Mr L Morrow)

12th Rifles. The Down men who were left, found themselves in the inferno once more in the German offensive of March 1918 – which nearly won the war. By June however, the German momentum had stalled, and the Allies, now aided by American troops, pressed forward.

The Down men moved back to Belgium, where they were involved in a series of gruelling, but successful offensives. On 11 November 1918 they were resting near Courtrai. The war was over.

Back to Down

Most of the Down men came home in early 1919. In the period after the Armistice most of their time was taken up in classes to prepare them for the return to civilian life, and in various recreational activities – especially sporting competitions.

What did the men return to? The land fit for heroes never materialised – jobs were hard to come by, and to many veterans it seemed that people were quick to forget.

Peace Day celebrations were held throughout Ulster in the summer of 1919. Festivities were mixed with sorrow. People remembered the dead, the wounded, those psychologically scarred or physically disabled for life. A support fund was established which would continue to assist soldiers and their families for a long time.

Ex-soldiers formed Old Comrade Associations (OCAs). Branches were set up throughout the Province, providing a source of friendship and support, and assisting in the organisation of remembrance events. One of the most active OCAs was the 13th RIR's. They held their last meeting in 1976.

Over 60 years earlier they left their quiet County Down roads and villages. The war was fought in foreign fields, but its effects were felt in the homes of Newry and Banbridge, Portaferry and Groomsport – and it echoes to this day.

Craig McGuicken is the Curator of the Somme Heritage Centre, Newtownards. In 2002 the Somme Heritage Centre produced an exhibition about the 13th Royal Irish Rifles which will be touring County Down until 2005.

13th RIR Old Comrades parading in Ballygowan in 1960 (Somme Heritage Centre Collection)

In Foreign Fields: Soldiers of Down in the Great War. The Down County Museum Collection

Noel Hogg and M Lesley Simpson

In January 2004 an exhibition about the Great War opened in Down County Museum. It was based on objects from our own collection but with text panels which had been produced as a travelling exhibition by the Somme Heritage Centre. The text focused on the 13th Battalion of the Royal Irish Rifles (13th RIR), who were largely raised from County Down. Written by Craig McGuicken, the text is included as a separate article in this yearbook. A computer interactive about 1916, featuring both the Battle of the Somme and the Easter Rising, lent by the Nerve Centre in Derry, further enhanced the exhibition. We are grateful to our colleagues in both of these organisations for their help. Preparation for the exhibition gave us the opportunity to research the material in our own collection for the first time and to prepare the following catalogue.

Ulster Volunteer Force, Ballynahinch contingent

Members of the Portaferry Company of Irish Volunteers, about 1914. In addition to the 30,000 Ulster Volunteers who fought in the First World War, about 30,000 members of the Irish Volunteers joined the British Army. Most of them served in the 16th (Irish) Division (Courtesy of the Ulster Museum)

Catalogue

Uniform and accessories

Tunic and belt from the uniform of Dr W W Glenny, Royal Army Medical Corp. The belt, known as a 'Sam Browne', was called after Sir S J Browne. After the war, Dr Glenny became a general practitioner in Warrenpoint.
DCM 1994-330
Given by Mr & Mrs J B Pyper, Belfast.

Tunic, buttons in Rifle Black, of Infantry Regiment, Rifle Brigade. Seven buttons still attached, 4 buttons missing. A wound stripe is attached to the left sleeve.
Army soft cap with stitching on the peak and band. Stamped inside 'Myers & Co 7 1918'. Two buttons attached but badge missing. This type of cap was issued from 1917. These items belonged to the donor's father, James Mc Bride.
DCM 2004-261, 262
Given by Mr J D McBride, Downpatrick.

A feature introduced on khaki uniforms during this period was battlefield identification insignia. Coloured 'patches' of cloth were attached to the upper arms, shoulder straps and the back of the jacket.[1] Neither of these tunics has any 'patches'. Wound stripes were introduced in 1916.

Army greatcoat. It has been cut down for re-use and has three buttons missing. It belonged to the donor's great uncle, Louis McKinstry.
DCM 2004-263
Given by Mr C McKinstry, Downpatrick.

Pair of khaki cloth puttees.
These belonged to Major David Mitchell Anderson, who was gazetted in August 1914 to the 5th Royal Irish Rifles. He served in France between March and June 1915 with the 2nd Battalion and was wounded at the Battle of Hooge. In 1917 he served with the 1st Battalion. In 1918 he was a Musketry Instructor and Staff Captain at Lahore in India. Major Anderson also served in World War Two, when he commanded the 9th Battery Ulster Searchlight Regiment (Supplementary Reserve) RA from 1938 to 1940. He was in France between 1939 and 1940.
DCM 2004-264
Given by Mrs Annie Donnan, Saintfield.

Puttees, worn by an American soldier.
DCM 1997-326
Patsy Mullen collection.

Pair of leather leg guards.
Sam Browne belt, leather, (part of this, which fits over the shoulder, is missing; many non-combatants wore the waist belt only).
These belonged to the donor's father, the Reverend Stuart Hall. He belonged to an organisation called 'Scottish Church Huts' and organised stores and taught driving around Deauville and Trauville in France during the Great War.
DCM 2004-265, 266
Given by Miss K M V Hall, Downpatrick.

Metal helmet, probably from the First World War.
DCM 1998-17
Given by Mr T Morrison, Downpatrick.

Five buttons, Royal Irish Rifles, 1901-21 period. 1.9 cm diam.
Collar badge, Royal Irish Rifles, pattern adopted 1912, for roll collar jacket. 5.2 x 3.5 cm. These items belonged to the donor's uncle, David Adams, who served in both World Wars.
DCM 1994-373, 1995-153
Given by Mr & Mrs A Johnston, Cloghy, Strangford.

Identity disc, J Hillard of Annadorn. 4.9 x 2.5 cm.
DCM 2004-200
Given by Mr Ciaran McNulty, Downpatrick

Enamel badge 'On War Service 1914', 2.5 cm diam. These badges were worn by young men carrying out war duties at home.
DCM 2004-234
Given by Mr D J Patterson, Carryduff, Belfast.

Weapons, ammunition and tools

Wooden trench club, used in silent night attacks to capture enemy soldiers. 33.5 cm long.
Leather water bottle, possibly German.

The Royal Engineers (Signals), 36th Ulster Division, on the Mall, Downpatrick, 1914. This group were based in the Old Gaol (now our museum) from November 1914 to June 1915, after being washed out of their tents at the Clandeboye camp

Gas mask in cylindrical container, German. Tin 15.2 cm high, 12 cm diam.
Bayonet, German. [2]
These items belonged to the donor's brother, Captain Ralph Parkinson-Cumine. The items of German origin may have been brought back as souvenirs.
DCM 1993-308 to 311
Given by Miss C Parkinson-Cumine, Killough.

Tent peg mallet, military issue.
DCM 2004-268
Given by Mr F B McKeown, Ballygowan.

Leather bandolier (ammunition belt) with 50 ammunition loops and three leather flaps. Three other leather flaps are missing. Possibly made by J & E Pullman of London.
Full flap leather holster.
Both these items belonged to the donor's uncle, Colour Sergeant Samuel Morrison (1869–1941) of Downpatrick.
DCM 2001-184, 185
Given by Mr John Morrison, Downpatrick.

Two brass timer heads from artillery shells. 8cm long, 7cm wide at base. These were found at the Somme battlefield by the donor's grandfather. He later died as a result of his war injuries.
DCM 2002-297
Given by Mr G Pell, Downpatrick.

Brass shell case, made into cap shape. Engraved 'Souvenir from Thiepval Somme, 1 July 1916'
DCM 2003-76
Given by Mrs Jill E Sampson, Killough.

Medals
Cap badge, Middlesex Regiment and military medals, awarded to Pte J Beha.
Badge 4 x 4.5 cm.
Boxed set of two medals:
British War Medal, 1914–1918
Victory Medal
DCM 1986-140, 1986-141/1, 2
Given by Mr R Morath, Newcastle.

Six military medals awarded to Robert McClurg (1894–1976) of Crossgar. [3]

British War Medal, 1914–1918 (Sgt R McClurg)
Victory Medal (Sgt R McClurg)
1914–1915 Star (Pte R McClurg)
Military Medal for Bravery in the Field (L/Cpl R McClurg)
Croix-de-Guerre
Defence Medal
Additional ribbons for medals.
Demob certificate of Sgt R McClurg, dated 1919.

Bob McClurg was born in Crossgar, one of twelve children. He became a joiner and worked on the Wallace estate, at Myra Castle. Colonel Wallace recruited him into the 5th Battalion, Royal Irish Rifles in 1915. He fought in the battle of the Somme in 1916 and was awarded the Croix-de-Guerre by the French and the Military Medal by the British for his bravery during this battle. Bob also served in the Home Guard during the Second World War. Back home, he received an award from parishioners at Teconnaught for rescuing a man working on the roof of the chapel.
DCM 1992-19, 24
Given by Mr Oliver Priestley, Corbally, Killyleagh.

Military medals, boxed set of four medals and ribbons awarded to J H Jordan, Royal Army Medical Corp. [4]
British War Medal, 1914–1918 (Major J H Jordan)
Victory Medal (Major J H Jordan)
1914–1915 Star (Lt J H Jordan)
Military Cross (Captain J H Jordan)
Two additional ribbons in box.
Letter from the War Office about the Military Cross awarded to J H Jordan (Captain), 1916.
Commission as Lieutenant in the Royal Army Medical Corp to John Herbert Jordan, 1915.
DCM 1995-76, 77, 1994-323
Given by the Estate of the late Walrond Clarke of Clough.

Medal ribbons on two metal bars (medals missing).
British War Medal, 1914–1918
Victory Medal
1914–1915 Star with rose for 1914 Star
Burma Star 1941–1945

Defence Medal 1939–1945
Long Service and Good Conduct Medal
War Medal, 1939–1945
Territorial Efficiency Medal
DCM 1995-100
Given by Mr & Mrs A Johnston, Strangford.

Seven military medals awarded to James Roulston, of Bright, Downpatrick. James enlisted in the Inniskilling Fusiliers in 1892. After serving in India and South Africa he left in 1913 but rejoined when the First World War began. He went on to serve in the Home Guard in World War Two.
India Medal, 1895 with bars Tirah 1897–98, Malakand 1897, Punjab Frontier 1897–98
Bar, Transvaal Orange Free State, from Queen's South Africa Medal (medal missing)
British War Medal, 1914–18
Victory Medal
1914–1915 Star
Defence Medal
Long Service and Good Conduct Medal
Badge, metal, for peaked cap, 'Inneskilling'.
DCM 1993-267/1-6
Given by Mrs E Montgomery, Dunmurry, Belfast.

Seven miniature dress medals and ribbons on bar
Distinguished Flying Cross (1918)
1939–1945 Star
The Atlantic Star
The Africa Star
The Italy Star
Defence Medal
The War Medal, 1939–1945
DCM 1996-120/1-7
Given by Mrs E Ash, Killyleagh.

German Iron Cross Medal, 1914.
DCM 1997-328
Patsy Mullen Collection.

Memorials and commemorative items
Grave marker. Wooden cross, 1.24 m high, 69.7 cm wide. 'In memory of Sapper John Malone Reg No 64005 121 Field Company RE Killed in action May 23 1916 Until the day break'. These temporary wooden crosses were later replaced by headstones.
Letter, dated 1924, from the Church Army, which

The Love Family of Scotch Street, Downpatrick. All eight sons served in the army in the First World War.
Top row, left to right:
'Mother'; Sergeant Walter Love served in the Royal Irish Rifles and was wounded at Neuve Chapelle; Sapper Samuel Love served in the Royal Engineers and was killed in France 8 April 1916; Corporal Thomas Love served in the Royal Engineers and was wounded in France; 'Father' (R J Love).
Bottom row, left to right:
Sergeant Major Joseph Love was in the 'C' Company of the 13th Battalion, Royal Irish Rifles and fought at the battle of the Somme in 1916. He had also served with the East Yorkshires in the Boer War; Corporal Robert James Love served with the Argyll and Sutherland Highlanders and had also been in the Boer War; David Love served with the Royal Irish Rifles and came with his regiment from India; Pioneer Sergeant George Love joined the Royal Irish Rifles and was wounded in France. After recovering in a French hospital he rejoined his unit and was killed on 30 September 1916; Sergeant John Love was in the 'C' Company of the 13th Battalion, Royal Irish Rifles and was one of the first to volunteer at the outbreak of war. He was killed at the battle of the Somme in 1916

accompanied the wooden cross, when it was sent to John's relatives.
Letter to John Malone, dated 1916.
9 million soldiers and up to 50 million civilians died in the Great War. This temporary grave marker and photograph of Sapper John Malone, from Downpatrick, reminds us of the individuals involved. John joined the 121st Royal Engineers and was killed in 1916. He is buried in Hamel Military Cemetery, Beaumont-Hamel, north-east France. The letter was written to him by his brother, not long before his death.
DCM 1984-106
Given by Mr Eric V Malone, Downpatrick.

Memorial plaque bearing the name Walter McAuley. 12 cm diam. Over one million were issued to the next of kin of those killed in the war.
DCM 1995-140
Given by Mr P Tomelty, Downpatrick.

Illuminated Roll of Honour[5] 'Employees of Drumaness Mills who have joined the Colours in defence of King and Country since the outbreak of War'. Produced by W E G Baird, Illuminators, Belfast. 39 x 53 cm.
DCM 1983-114
(see photograph, p 41)
From the Dan Rice Memorial Hall, Drumaness.

Boxed replica of *The Lusitania Medal*, the original of which was struck in Germany. Medal 5.2 cm diam; box 8 x 7.8 cm. These were reproduced in England as a propaganda measure, as many civilians were killed when the boat was torpedoed in 1915. However, it was being used to carry weapons at the time, despite assertions to the contrary.
DCM 1998-122
Given by Mrs M C Douglas, Newcastle.

Framed picture on glass, of the *Lusitania*. Picture 17.1 x 17.7 cm; frame 23 x 23 cm.
Ticket for the voyage to New York on the *Lusitania*, dated 1 December 1914.
DCM 1996-74 & 76
Bequest from the late Mr R J Edgar, Ballyhosset, Downpatrick.

Metal match box holder, top inscribed 'Les Halles The Cloth Halls 1914', base inscribed 'Les Halles Ypres 1918'; text on side 'Site de Guerre Belgique War sites Belgium'. 5.5 x 3.7 x 1.7 cm.
DCM 1986-387
Given by Mr & Mrs D J Patterson, Carryduff.

'Princess Mary's Christmas Box', brass box for tobacco and cigarettes, engraved 'M M Imperium Britannicum Christmas 1914 Servia, France, Belgium, Japan, Russia, Montenegro'. Contains empty packet of tobacco marked 'Her Royal Highness The Princess Mary's Fund 1914', Christmas card and photograph. 12.7 x 8.3 x 2.9 cm.
DCM 1994-54
Given by Mrs E Cochrane, Downpatrick.

Postcards
See article by Madeleine McAllister in this volume for embroidered postcards.

Seven First World War period postcards:
'I'm thinking of you at Saintfield'
'I do hope they'll fit!'
'Are we downhearted? No!' Postmark 1914.
'Comrades in Arms'
'To my husband at the front'
'Tip-Top Tipperary Mary'
'There's a long, long trail'

DCM 1983-86, 2004-300 to 305
The James Seeds Collection.

Five First World War period postcards:
'Army Service Corps'
'All the girls want souvenir buttons – I won't part with any more!' Postmark 1916.
'I'm on the lookout for someone in'
'Field Marshall Sir John French'
'For the King, for the Flag, and the dear Homeland'.
DCM 1983-106/2, 3, 5; 2004-156
Given by Mr and Mrs F Dornan, Newcastle.

Four postcards, Official War Photographs (*Daily Mail* War Pictures):
'The Glorious First of July 1916'
'Wounded Tommy to the photographer "I'm not a German!"'
'After the first cavalry charge, July 1916'
'Firing a heavy howitzer in France'
DCM 2004-1 to 4
Purchase.

German card, 'Feldwache beim Abkochen'. Postmark 1915.
DCM 2004-150
Purchase.

Postcard of Palace Barracks, Holywood. Postmark 1918.
Two postcards of Clandeboye Camp.
'Off to Clandeboye camp'.
DCM 2004-153 to155, 2004-300
Acquired by exchange / purchase.

Four postcards, Ballykinlar Camp. [6]
DCM 2003-48 to 49, 2004-163
Acquired by exchange.

Two postcards:
'Brave Little Belgium'
'Cavalry manoeuvres in the Long Valley'
DCM 2004-306, 307
Given by Mrs Florence Coffey, Cluntagh, Crossgar.

Propaganda card, 'The World and the Devil'.
DCM 2004-308
Given by Mr R Anderson, Banbridge.

One card with Union Flag applied to front, sent at Christmas.
DCM 1993-441
Given by Mr S G McCracken, Clough.

Three First World War period postcards:
'To my Dear Son at the Front'
'Good news from the Front'
'HMS Dove'
DCM 2004-309 to 311
Anonymous donation.

Cigarette cards
Album, produced by Gallaher Ltd containing various cigarette cards. Signed James Seeds and dated 1912 inside front cover. Those relating to the First World War are as follows:
Army Corp and Divisional Signs, issued 1924 and 1925, complete series of 150
Colonial & Indian Army Badges, issued 1917, complete series of 25
War Decorations and Medals, issued 1927, 80 cards from a series of 90.
Above three sets issued by John Player & Sons.
Allied Army Leaders, issued 1917, 10 cards from a series of 50
Military Motors, issued 1916, 10 cards from a series of 50
Recruiting Posters, issued 1915, 9 cards from a series of 12
Above three sets issued by W D & H O Wills.
The Great War Series, issued 1915, 9 cards from a series of 100
Issued by Gallaher Ltd.
DCM 2004-299
The James Seeds Collection.

Books, newspapers and other documents
Booklet, *Black Book of the War*. Full text of the seven official reports on German atrocities in France and Belgium. Published by the *Daily Chronicle*, undated.
DCM 1986-267
Given by D J McNeill, Downpatrick.

Book, *Infantry Training*, 1914. This belonged to the donor's grandfather.
DCM 2004-282
Given by Mr David Clements, Downpatrick.

The following newspapers have references to the war:
The Northern Whig, 3 July 1916, 7 July 1916, 8 July 1916.
DCM 1990-14/1, 14/2, 14/3
Given by Miss Jean Jennings, Inch, Downpatrick.

Daily Mirror, 26 October 1916.
DCM 1987-41
Given by Mr Stephen Dowd, Downpatrick.

The General Advertiser and Local Government Record, 24 November 1917.
DCM 2004-313

Belfast Newsletter, 11 November 1918.
DCM 2004-312

The Derry Standard, 19 March 1915.
The Londonderry Sentinel, 31 October 1916, 2 November 1916, 22 February 1917, 26 April 1917, 28 June 1917, 26 July 1917, 19 October 1919.
DCM 1990-20/2 to 4
Anonymous donation.

The Belfast Telegraph, 11 November 1918
DCM 2002-47
Given by Mr J Potter, Strangford

Certificate, The National Egg Collection, presented to Miss Margaret Glenny Tweedie of Becknamullagh, Dromore.
DCM 2004-283
Given by Mr David Tweedie, Newtownards.

Two calendars:
Calendar, 1914, Ulster Volunteer Force 37.7 x 25.2 cm.
Calendar, 1915 East Down Unionist Association. 35 x 25 cm.
These were found behind a dresser in the donors' house.
DCM 1990-41/1&2
Given by Ms M L Simpson and Dr B G Scott, Balloo, Killinchy.

Certificate, dated 23 April 1917. Awarded to Rifleman Richard McCracken 13th Royal Irish Rifles, 36th Ulster Division, for conspicuous gallantry on 1 July 1916 at Thiepval.
DCM 2004-284
Donor's name withheld.

Programme of events for Peace Day Celebration in Downpatrick, 19 July 1919.
DCM 1996-186
Given by Mr E V Malone, Downpatrick.

Ration book, in the donor's maiden name, Joan L Harris, stamp on back cover dated 7 November 1918.
DCM 1994-439
Given by Mrs J L Meneely, Newcastle.

Works of Art
Two crayon drawings by William Conor.
A soldier in the Royal Irish Rifles at Newcastle Camp, 1916 (see front cover). Although he is un-named, he represents the thousands of ordinary Irishmen who enlisted in the armed services. 33 x 53 cm.
Major William James Hall (1866–1917) of Narrow Water Castle, at Donard Lodge Camp, Newcastle, 1917. 34 x 63 cm (see p 41)
DCM 1992-15, 1996-35
Purchased with assistance from the County Down Museum Trust and Northern Ireland Museums Council.

Watercolour painting, signed AP, of Ellen Constance, Countess Kilmorey, dressed in nurse's uniform, about 1914. 58 x 53 cm.
DCM 2004-168
Purchased with the assistance of the Northern Ireland Museums Council

Lesley Simpson is Keeper of Collections at Down County Museum. Noel Hogg has been a volunteer at the Museum for 9 years.

Notes and references
1. Mike Chappell, *British Battle Insignia* 1, 1914 – 1918, Men at Arms Series, 2000.
2. See 'Swords and Pikes' by Noel Hogg in *Down Survey*, 1999.
3. See Willie Crea, 'Bob McClurg, soldier from Crossgar' in *Lecale Miscellany*, vol 17 (1999) for further details.
4. For other related material, including a portrait of John Herbert Jordan, see 'From the Cradle to the Grave' by Madeleine McAllister and Lesley Simpson in *Down Survey*, 1999.
5. See article by Jane Leonard, p 55.
6. See 'Volunteers at the World's End' by Philip Orr in *Down Survey*, 2002.

Acknowledgements
We would like to thank Tom Wylie, formerly Assistant Keeper, Department of History, Ulster Museum, for his assistance with this catalogue.

Living History event at Down County Museum, January 2004. Members of Northern Period Productions are pictured in the exhibition gallery in front of a photograph of Sapper John Malone of Downpatrick, who was killed on 23 May 1916. The wooden cross was the original marker from his grave

Crayon drawing by William Conor. Major William James Hall (1866–1917), of Narrow Water Castle

Cigarette card 'Remember Belgium'

Roll of Honour from Drumaness Mill, from the Dan Rice Memorial Hall, Drumaness

Two Views of The Mall, Downpatrick, in Down County Museum

Eileen Black

Paintings of local views are always an asset to any museum collection. That there are two showing The Mall, Downpatrick, in Down County Museum's holdings is not only a double bonus but makes for a fascinating artistic comparison. The earlier of the two works, hitherto catalogued as by an unknown artist, probably dates to around 1850. By good fortune, a clue to the identity of its anonymous creator lies in a picture in the Ulster Museum's History collection: *View of the Cathedral and Mall, Downpatrick*, painted by the County Down artist James Glen Wilson in 1850. Both the Down County Museum and Ulster Museum works are remarkably close in composition and technique. Both show the scene from a virtually identical angle; furthermore, the handling of the paint, especially in the depiction of the trees and sky, is similar in the two pictures, as is the treatment of the various figures. In addition, that soldiers are included in both is in keeping with Wilson's fondness for such details. For these reasons, an attribution to him is entirely appropriate. Of the two paintings, the Down County Museum version is the more finished, in the greater attention paid to the architectural detail of the buildings and in the inclusion of the fences leading up to the cathedral.

Wilson is something of an enigma in the art history of the north.[1] Highly talented as a painter of local views and seascapes, his life prior to the spring of 1852, when he joined the Royal Navy as a ship's artist, remains frustratingly cloaked in obscurity. According to his death certificate of 6 August 1863, issued in Australia, he was born in Ireland in 1827, the son of James William Wilson, gentleman and Elizabeth Glen. Regrettably, the document fails to mention a specific location within the country. Nevertheless, it is possible to draw a few reasonably sound conclusions from it. His background was probably prosperous, as his father was a gentleman, that is, a man of independent means, perhaps inherited wealth. It seems likely, furthermore, that the family were of Ulster Presbyterian stock, judging by the Scottish overtones of the name. A reference in a leading Belfast newspaper, the *Northern Whig* of 13 January 1852, states that he was a native of County Down. Although it has proved impossible to verify this so far – Wilson is an extremely common name in the northern counties – it seems probable that he was indeed born somewhere in the north and perhaps in County Down, as the paper claimed.

The Mall, Downpatrick (c. 1850), hitherto catalogued as by an unknown artist, oil on board 17 x 22.8 cm. Now attributed to James Glen Wilson (1827–63) (DCM 1996-25)

View of the Cathedral and Mall, Downpatrick (1850), by James Glen Wilson (1827–63), oil on canvas 22.8 x 30.9 cm (Ulster Museum)

His artistic background is also shrouded in mystery. The earliest known reference to him as an artist occurs in the *Northern Whig* of 23 October 1849, in an advertisement for a lithograph showing the sectarian disturbance at Dolly's Brae, County Down on 12 July of that year. The print, published by Marcus Ward & Co, was apparently taken from a sketch made on the spot by Wilson, who was described in the advertisement as being self-taught. Whilst this may have been true at the time of publication, it seems likely that he received some formal training at a later date, namely, at the Belfast Government School of Design during the early 1850s. That he attended the school is stated in a Belfast exhibition catalogue of 1870, which claimed that he had once been a pupil.[2] Unfortunately, there are no records of the establishment and existing evidence, such as newspaper reports, contains no mention of him. Opened in December 1849, the school was geared mainly to producing imaginative designers for the local linen industry and provided public classes for artisans and private tuition for ladies and gentlemen. Given Wilson's presumably comfortable background, he may perhaps have availed himself of the latter classes during 1850 and 1851.

Although there are so few concrete facts regarding Wilson's early life, one thing is certain: he was painting around County Down and Belfast between 1849 and early 1852. The Dolly's Brae and Downpatrick views of 1849 and 1850 have already been alluded to. That his travels also took him to the small County Down village of Ardglass has recently been revealed in the discovery of two scenes of the spot, one of which is dated 1850, in a private collection in England.[3] A third landscape in the same collection may perhaps depict somewhere in the neighbourhood or elsewhere in the north. There are also three Belfast views in the Ulster Museum, namely, *The First Lock at Stranmillis*, painted in 1850, *Belfast Quay*, which dates from 1851 and Wilson's masterpiece and best-known work, *Emigrant Ship leaving Belfast*, executed in 1852. A fourth view of Belfast – *Belfast Harbour, Ferry Steps* – painted in 1851, is owned by the Belfast Harbour Commissioners. These pictures, ten in all, including the newly attributed work in Down County Museum, comprise his known body of northern scenes.

In comparison with his early years, a good deal of information is available on Wilson's career after March 1852, when he joined the Royal Navy as a member of the survey vessel HMS *Herald*, due to make an expedition to the South Seas. *Herald's* Muster Books record his rank as being that of subordinate officer and his position as 'artist borne as clerk'.[4] Besides having to produce paintings and drawings on the journey (of which there are some hundreds in a private collection in

James Glen Wilson (1827–63) in naval uniform, taken at some point between March 1852 and April 1856 (Private Collection, London)

London and in the Hydrographic Department of the Ministry of Defence at Taunton, as well as several in collections in Australia), he was equipped with a camera, to take 'representations of a very superior description'.[5] Unfortunately, none of the photographs can be located with the exception of two: that of Wilson illustrated here and one of *Herald's* crew. The expedition, which lasted almost nine years with periodic visits to Sydney, *Herald's* temporary base, explored and surveyed the area embraced by New South Wales, New Zealand, the Kermadec group of islands, Tonga, Fiji, the New Hebrides and New Caledonia. *Herald* finally returned to England in May 1861.

Wilson, however, was not with the ship, having left the navy in late 1858 or early 1859 to settle in Australia. His reason for this was probably based on romance, as he had fallen in love with a young woman from Sydney, Margaret Bennett Moore. The couple were married on 3 February 1859 in St John's Church of England Church in Parramatta, a suburb of the city. The following month he took up a position as surveyor with the New South

Wales Department of Lands. His first year in employment was spent in the south coast area of New South Wales. In January 1860 he moved to Molong, a small town still in its infancy, about two hundred miles west of Sydney. This became his base for the rest of his life. In January 1863 his health broke down and by the following month, he was unable to work, the cause being 'an acute attack of dysentery, complicated with chronic inflammation of the stomach'.[6] By June he had rheumatic fever, from which he never recovered. He died on 6 August 1863, aged thirty-six and was buried in Molong. All traces of his grave have since disappeared, as he was buried in the town's old cemetery, which ceased to exist in about 1930. Sadly, there is no information regarding his wife thereafter. Family records state that she died in Kent in 1904 but this cannot be established. She, too, therefore, remains something of an enigma for the historian. Such lack of detail helps compound the mystery surrounding her husband, one of the most gifted artists produced by the north of Ireland in the nineteenth century.

Much less is known of the painter of the second and later view of The Mall – Thomas Semple. According to local street directories, a person of this name (occasionally spelt 'Sempill') worked in Little May Street and Corporation Street, Belfast, as a marine painter, decorator, gilder and picture frame maker between 1854 and 1870. Recent research has revealed that he had a son, Thomas, likewise an artist, as indicated by the latter's death notice in the *Larne Weekly Reporter* of 26 December 1874: 'December 18, at Larne, Mr. Thomas Semple, son of Mr Thomas Semple, Corporation – street, Belfast, aged 32 years. The deceased laboured for many years in Larne as an artist, and was generally respected for his unobtrusiveness'.[7] Whichever of the two – father or son – painted the view of The Mall, is uncertain. However, as Semple Senior is described as a marine painter and obviously specialized as such, an attribution to Semple Junior would appear the more likely option. Despite living in Larne, it seems probable that he visited other parts of the north, including Downpatrick and Belfast. The distances are not great.

Whoever painted the scene, which is signed

The Mall,
Downpatrick
(1863) by Thomas
Semple, oil on
canvas 60 x 92 cm.
Probably painted
by Thomas Semple
Junior (1842–74)
rather than Thomas
Semple Senior (fl.
1854–70) (DCM
1986–436)

The late William
Dougherty's Fowl
Stores (1869) by
Thomas Semple, oil
on canvas 59.3 x 89
cm. By the same
hand as that of The
Mall, Downpatrick,
that is, probably
Thomas Semple
Junior (1842–74)
(Ulster Museum)

and dated 1863 – Semple Senior or Junior – the standard of the work indicates that the artist had received little if any training, as the picture is decidedly primitive in appearance. There is, for example, little sense of atmosphere or depth and the figures in the foreground seem overly large. The perspective of the buildings is also somewhat crude, especially in the depiction of the gaol, to the extreme right. Interestingly, there is another street scene, clearly by the same hand as the view of The Mall, in the Ulster Museum's History collection: *The late William Dougherty's Fowl*

Stores. Signed and dated as by Thomas Semple, 1869, it too is probably by Semple Junior. Equally primitive in execution to the Downpatrick scene, it depicts Dougherty's fowl stores in Belfast's May Street. Both the painting of the figures and the rendering of the architectural details on the building is extremely crude. Like the view of The Mall, its worth lies in its local historical value and not in its artistic merit. These two street scenes, together with a portrait of Robert Burns owned by the Belfast Burns Club, comprise the only known works by Thomas Semple.

Though the paintings of Thomas Semple Senior and Junior continue to puzzle, no such quandaries surround the works of an artist who almost certainly belonged to the same family and was possibly Thomas Senior's brother – Joseph Semple. Whilst there are few concrete facts about his life save that he was a marine painter, decorator, gilder and picture frame maker of Corporation Street, Belfast and that he flourished between 1863 and 1878, he has fortunately left a substantial body of work, mainly ship portraits (a number of examples are also signed as 'Sempill'). About forty paintings by him are known to date, in public and private collections in Canada, the United States, Britain and Ireland.[8] Of his pictures in the latter country, four are represented in the Belfast Harbour Commissioners' collection, small works depicting various iron paddle steamers which plied the routes between Belfast and Ardrossan, Fleetwood and Liverpool.[9] The standard of his art, competent rather than exciting, is nevertheless decidedly higher than that of his probable relative, Thomas Semple. Taken together, works by the two men provide a fascinating glimpse of another art world in the north, that of the semi-amateur painter who did not aspire to 'high' art but turned out images for a less sophisticated clientele and earned extra income from decorating and framing.

The scene depicted in both views of The Mall could be said to be the trademark of Downpatrick, so well known is the image of the cathedral and adjacent buildings. To the left are the Southwell Charity Schools and Almshouses, built by Edward Southwell in 1733 to provide almshouses for six men and six women, with schools for ten poor children.[10] One of the best early Georgian buildings in Ulster, its design is typical of Irish Palladianism. Dominating the background is Down Cathedral, restored from the early 1790s and consecrated in 1818.[11] To the right are The Judges' Lodgings, an elegant pair of Regency-style houses erected at some point after 1835, whilst in the right foreground can be seen the late

eighteenth century gaol, shown with soldiers on guard duty in both of Wilson's works.[12] With poetic appropriateness, this latter building, restored and opened in stages as Down County Museum between 1981 and 1991, is now the custodian of County Down's heritage.

Dr. Eileen Black is a Curator of Fine Art in the Ulster Museum, Belfast. Amongst her numerous publications are catalogues of the museum's Irish oil paintings, 1572–1900 and of the fine art collections of Queen's University and the Belfast Harbour Commissioners.

Notes and references
1. For details of Wilson's career, see Eileen Black, *James Glen Wilson (1827–1863): Landscape and Marine Painter*, exhibition catalogue, Ulster Museum, 3-30 September 1980. Also by the author: 'James Glen Wilson (1827–1863): an Irish Artist in Australia', *Familia*, vol 2, no 3, 1987; 'James Glen Wilson of Ireland and Australia: an enigmatic artist', *Irish Arts Review*, Yearbook 1990–91; 'James Glen Wilson' in Joan Kerr (ed), *The Dictionary of Australian Artists* (Melbourne, 1992); *A Catalogue qf the Permanent Collection: 4: Irish Oil Paintings, 1831–1900*, Ulster Museum, 1997.
2. *Belfast and North of Ireland Workman's exhibition*, Ulster Hall, 17 May – 4 June 1870. Wilson's *Emigrant Ship* was no 70 in the show.
3. Ulster Museum records.
4. Black, 1980, p 5.
5. Ibid., p 7.
6. Ibid., p 11.
7. Information on Thomas Semple Junior from George Rutherford (letters of 10, 27 May 2000). I am grateful to Mr Rutherford for these details.
8. Information from Samuel Davidson (letter of 19 November 2001).
9. See Eileen Black, *Paintings, Sculptures and Bronzes in the Collection of The Belfast Harbour Commissioners, 1983*, pp 40, 41, 99. Additional information supplied by the author.
10. See *List of Historic Buildings, Groups of Buildings, Areas of Architectural Importance in the Town of Downpatrick*, Ulster Architectural Heritage Society, 1970, pp 9, 17.
11. For a scholarly and fascinating account of the cathedral, see J. Frederick Rankin, *Down Cathedral:The Church of Saint Patrick of Down* (Belfast, 1997). See also Ulster Architectural Heritage Society Downpatrick List (n 10), pp 7, 13, 14.
12. Ulster Architectural Heritage Society Downpatrick List (n 10), pp 10, 17.

Embroidered Postcards of the First World War

Madeleine McAllister

Some of the most touching reminders of the First World War are the embroidered silk postcards sent by soldiers in France and Belgium to their family and friends at home. These delicate pieces of card and embroidered silk have often been carefully preserved and Down County Museum is lucky to have several in its collection.

Typically the cards are made of a piece of fine translucent silk, embroidered and mounted on a backing card, usually 90 x 140mm (3$\frac{1}{2}$ x 5$\frac{1}{2}$ inches). The embroidered design is surrounded by a 'frame' of embossed card. Some are made with a little flap to form a pocket so that a card or message can be tucked inside. The designs are embroidered in brightly coloured silks, and it is the variety and themes of these designs that make the cards so interesting.

Many of the designs feature sentimental greetings to friends and family at home, for example: 'A kiss from France', one with flowers and doves, another with pansies, roses and a fan; 'To my dear mother', one with pansies for thoughts, another with roses and the French and British flags. There are cards for birthdays, Christmas and Easter, which often include a patriotic message. A Christmas card shows a butterfly with wings embroidered with the British

Two embroidered postcards from a collection originally from a house in Newcastle

flag, while an Easter card has a basket of eggs in the colours of the Allied flags (Britain, France, Belgium and Russia), and an English rose, a Scottish thistle and a four leaved clover, probably intended as an Irish shamrock. Interestingly, the border on this card is embossed with a Christmas design of holly and mistletoe.

Many cards have the theme of the unity of the Allies and their fight for liberty portrayed in various ingenious ways. One depicts flags of France and Britain tied together and entitled 'United in Liberty', another has the flags of the Allies combined to form a cross, 'The Cross of the Allies'. A card with the message 'Greetings from France' is interesting in that it shows the flags of Britain, France, and America. This clearly dates from the last years of the war, after America joined the Allies.

Postcards which showed regimental badges or emblems were popular, for example the Royal Engineers and the Royal Army Medical Corps, which also incorporates the symbol of the Red Cross.

There is one very unusual card in the collection, on which a little spray of dried grass seed heads, dyed red, green and blue, is fixed to the card by an

Two embroidered postcards from a collection originally from a house in Newcastle

48

embroidered bouquet of flowers, coloured red, blue and white, and entitled 'Flowers of France, Gathered for you'.

Embroidered silk postcards first appeared towards the end of the nineteenth century, but it was during the First World War that they reached the peak of their popularity. Hand-embroidered as a cottage industry by French and Belgian women in towns, villages and refugee camps, they were made specifically for soldiers to send home. Working on a rough assembly line basis, card manufacturers from Paris would send out long strips of silk pre-printed with the design for up to twenty-five cards. When completed the strips were returned to the factory to be cut up and mounted. The quality of the embroidery on the cards can be quite variable, but most have been done by highly-skilled needlewomen, who were very poorly paid for their labours. The cards were then sold quite cheaply through YMCA shops and other similar outlets. They were mostly sold with a waxed paper cover or envelope for posting, though few if any of these are known to survive. The cards were clearly intended as a memento or a little gift, as many do not have hand written messages on the back. What messages there are, are generally written in pencil and are very short. For example the reverse of 'Flowers of France' reads 'Miss Swail, just a card to let you know I have not forgotten you, as ever, your friend Mac'.

It is estimated that over ten million of these cards were made during the First World War, though their popularity rapidly declined afterwards. Many thousands were kept and treasured, surely often as a memento of someone who did not return from the trenches. Now these seemingly flimsy pieces of brightly coloured silk are an enduring symbol of hope from those who endured the horrors of war.

Catalogue
'Greetings from France'. Message on reverse dated 16 November 1918.
DCM 1990-39
Given by Mrs Elizabeth Fleming, Coniamstown, Downpatrick.

ASC (Badge of the Army Service Corp).
DCM 2004-321
Given by Mr G Williams, Donaghadee.

'United for Liberty'
'Easter'. Message on reverse dated 20 March 1918.
DCM1986-493/1& 2
Given by Mrs M Jardine, Saintfield.

'The Cross of the Allies'.
DCM1983-105/15
Given by Mr & Mrs O'Hanlon, Downpatrick.

Embroidered postcard with a message on the reverse dated 20 March 1918

'Greetings from France My thoughts are with you'
DCM 2004-336
Anonymous donation.

'Flowers of France Gathered for you'
DCM 2004-337
Anonymous donation.

'Happy Christmas'
'Merry Christmas'
'Christmas Greetings'
'Happy Birthday'
'Birthday Greetings'
'To my dear mother' (2)
'A kiss from France' (2)
'Will soon be home'
'God be with you til we meet again'
'God save the King'
'For King and Country'
'RE Royal Engineers'
'RAMC' (2)
Embroidered, no text
Originally from a house in Newcastle.
DCM 2004-322 to 335
Purchase.

Madeleine McAllister is Assistant Keeper of Collections at Down County Museum.

Embroidered postcard with a message on the reverse dated 16 November 1918

'Flowers of France Gathered for you'

Memorials to the Great War in County Down, 1914–1939

Jane Leonard

Introduction

The most significant memorial on the Western Front to those from Ulster who died at the Somme evokes a landscape that is forever Down. The Ulster Tower at Thiepval in Northern France was unveiled by Field Marshal Sir Henry Wilson, in November 1921. It replicates Helen's Tower at Clandeboye, where the 36th (Ulster) Division trained in the opening months of the war. No collective tribute to the dead of Down was erected at home. While a wide range of communal and individual monuments in towns and villages brought home remembrance of the county's losses, few convey the character of war service as powerfully as the Thiepval Tower, which perpetuates both the friendships forged in training and the soldier's longing for home.[1]

This article introduces the rich heritage of war memorials throughout Down. Memorials are classified by those responsible for their erection: local authorities, churches, schools, clubs, firms, fraternities, surviving comrades and the communities of particular districts. Such a classification also helps to identify communities that did not erect tributes.[2]

In some respects, the commemorative landscape of County Down after the Great War is similar to parts of Britain or Australia, except for the extra dimension of fraternal memorials and the extent to which the remembrance of the war was politically divisive. This article focuses on inter-war commemorative projects, and therefore does not explore the impact in Down of the recent reclamation by Irish nationalists of the legacy of the Great War.

Local authority memorials

From 1914 onwards, many organisations maintained active service lists. Throughout the war, these were proudly read out at annual general meetings, church services, school prize days and other ceremonial occasions. Some local councils commissioned elaborate illuminated scrolls, recording the contribution of an entire town or area. Such tributes served to boost morale, stimulate recruitment and refute the suggestion that the community was not doing its bit. The bereaved and those left at home would be cheered by such a civic salute to their relatives.

During 1915, rolls of honour were commissioned by the Urban District Councils in Newry and Newcastle and by the Town Commissioners in Downpatrick. The most elaborate was Newry's, launched in late April, with an illuminated cover depicting the town's arms and the Allied flags. Recording the names, addresses, ranks, units and service numbers of 867 citizens, it confirmed the scale of participation in each of the town's wards. The roll was compiled by the town clerk with the help of the local RIC. Unionist and nationalist politicians and bands, along with clergy from all denominations, attended the unveiling. Speakers included a Belgian refugee priest while the repertoire included several national anthems, *Tipperary* and *The Minstrel Boy*. After the war, the roll was preserved by the British Legion in Newry.[3]

Over 100 names were submitted for the list displayed at the entrance to the Newcastle Council offices from the autumn of 1915 onwards. Among them was that of Pietro Biagioni, a pre-war confectioner recovering from frost-bite contracted while serving with the 38th Italian infantry. Downpatrick's list was intended for the local library. The various Protestant churches had forwarded their records by November 1915 but delays in obtaining details of Catholic servicemen meant the list was not approved for printing until February 1916.

Few local authorities commissioned permanent district memorials once the war ended. District memorials, as shown later, were generally secured through voluntary committees and were then handed into the care of local councils. The

Banbridge statue was handed over to the council immediately after the 1923 unveiling, as was responsibility for a framed list of 882 who had served, placed in the local library.[4] The council was also given the balance of the funds to be used for maintaining the memorial. Until the status of war memorials under local authority care was resolved under legislation of 1923, councils occasionally declined this responsibility. In 1920, Moira Rural Council refused a request to take over the newly dedicated obelisk in Dollingstown.

Church memorials

Post-war tributes in bronze, marble or stained glass were erected by most Church of Ireland, Presbyterian, Non-Subscribing Presbyterian, Methodist and Unitarian congregations in Down. The names of the fallen usually took precedence over survivors. Otherwise, the order of recording varied: names might be listed alphabetically, by military rank or standing in the community, by date of joining up or by unit.

Horace's celebrated maxim, *Dulce et Decorum Est Pro Patria Mori*, concluded the inscription on a plaque in Bryansford Church of Ireland, erected in 1920 to honour nine war dead. As well as mourning losses, church memorials also celebrated peace and embraced the survivors. When Ballyculter Church of Ireland held a welcome-home function in August 1919, the rector presented twelve veterans with a gold medal and a Bible containing each man's photograph and war record. The planned memorial, he announced, would commemorate how their 'strong hands and brave hearts had prevented the fair fields of Down from being ravaged and made a shambles like Belgium and Northern France'. A more muted tribute, perhaps reflecting the passage of time since the armistice, featured on the celtic cross, erected by Craigavad Church of Ireland in 1930, 'to those who dwelt with us in friendship and in faith. They died in war that we might live in peace.'

The aesthetic function was usually favoured over the utilitarian, though some Presbyterian churches opted for Victory pipe organs. Congregational windows usually featured regimental crests, the Burning Bush (if Presbyterian) and other Biblical scenes. In Ballygowan, the window erected in the Presbyterian Church was stated in one church publication to represent a Knight of Ulster with celtic borders, though a newspaper report described it as a classic St Michael.

Whose war service was commemorated? Most memorials recorded the names of soldiers, sailors and airmen. Merchant seamen were less commonly included, and civilian victims were rarely commemorated. A rare exception was Drumbo Church of Ireland, where a plaque erected in March 1916 remembered Walter Dawson Mitchell and his infant son, Walter, both drowned on the *Lusitania*.

Whereas Presbyterian and Methodist plaques usually listed female nurses and Red Cross workers, this was less common on Anglican tributes. The service of women in other spheres including munitions rarely featured. The illuminated roll of honour in Dromore Cathedral was unusually detailed. As well as listing seven female munitions workers and four nurses (including one who died), it also identified which soldiers were prisoners of war, gassed, shell-shocked or missing. The stained glass window to the congregation's fallen was unusual in giving precedence to a nurse, Elizabeth Watson.[5]

The records of memorial committees are crucial to documenting the debates over design and inclusion. Ballygilbert Presbyterian Church near Crawfordsburn offers a fascinating case-study. One prominent member of its congregation was Fred Crawford, the leading UVF gunrunner of 1914. Though he had not seen overseas service in the war, the committee wanted to include him as he had trained a reserve battalion of the Royal Irish Rifles (RIR). However, the liberal minister, Reverend William Orr, 'strongly objected' to this. Orr was moved to Waterford in 1922 but his concerns were upheld and Crawford did not feature when the plaque to survivors was unveiled in 1923.[6]

Occasionally, tributes to all local Protestants were sited in Anglican churchyards. Thus at Inch, the Church of Ireland has an indoor plaque to twelve parishioners killed in the war and an outdoor granite wall tablet to thirty-nine local servicemen of all Protestant denominations (mostly estate workers at Finnebrogue). The outdoor tablet somewhat confusingly urged that 'all ye who pass by remember with gratitude the men from the parish who served their King and Country in the great war'. Similarly, an outdoor column to local Protestants killed in the war stands in the grounds of Maralin (Magheralin) Church of Ireland near Lurgan. By contrast, the stone obelisk in the grounds of St John's Church of Ireland, although inscribed 'to the memory of the following residents of Moira who fell in the war', in fact lists only parishioners. It is thus crucial to examine unveiling reports in order to identify exactly which community or communities are being commemorated on such monuments. One historian, in claiming that the rifleman erected in the grounds of Mourne Presbyterian Church in Kilkeel commemorates the entire war dead of the town, has construed its location as excluding bereaved Catholics: 'a clear public statement indeed'. In repeating this claim, an historical geographer considered that this siting, 'in Kilkee (sic), Co Down, inevitably conveyed a sense of distance from acts of commemoration among Ulster Catholics.' The Kilkeel statue, unveiled in 1923, in fact honours only the dead of that particular congregation.[7]

No memorials appear to have been erected in the county's Catholic churches, echoing the paucity of such tributes throughout Ireland. In some parishes, those on war service were prayed for in lists read out at weekly Mass.[8] Catholic servicemen were listed in a roll of honour printed in the programme of the Killylcagh Red Cross Sale and Fete, held in October 1918. It recorded 98 Presbyterians, 66 Anglicans, one Baptist and 81 Catholics who had enlisted. Of those killed, 13 were Presbyterian, 8 were Anglican and 8 were Catholic.[9] Official war graves and dedications on family headstones in cemeteries provide further reminders of Catholic bereavement. Names recorded on the Keenan family headstone in Downpatrick Catholic Cemetery include Corporal P K Keenan, 1st RIR, killed at Neuve Chapelle in May 1915, and Francis J Keenan, 14th RIR (YCVs), killed at Thiepval on 1 July 1916.[10] Other

reminders include the inter-war tradition of Armistice Day Masses (held in Newry, Rostrevor and Warrenpoint) or parochial poppy collections (as happened in Kirkcubbin and Loughbrickland).

Church monuments were also commissioned by officers' next of kin or by their surviving comrades. The most elaborate family tributes were stained glass windows. A full size depiction of St George in Ardglass Church of Ireland commemorates Major George Gaffikin who was killed leading the West Belfast battalion of the RIR into action on the first day of the Somme. The window was dedicated a year after he was killed. On the Ards peninsula, a window in Holy Trinity Church of Ireland, Ballywalter, remembers Captain Andrew Mulholland, son of Lord Dunleath, who was killed in November 1914 while serving with the Irish Guards. Side portraits of St Michael and St George flank guardsmen advancing through No Man's Land. Unveiled in 1921, this window is one of very few examples in Ireland to depict the Western Front. Like Gaffikin's, it was made by the London finn of Heaton, Butler and Baynes.

What enhances the immediacy of the Mulholland window is that his original grave marker hangs underneath. When replaced by the permanent headstones of the Imperial War Graves Commission, thousands of these wooden crosses were returned to next of kin during the 1920s. For a small fee, families could bring home to Down the part of the Western Front that was most precious to them. Dispatching a cross (now in the Down County Museum, see page 41) in 1924 to the family of John Malone, a Downpatrick soldier killed in May 1916, a Church Army official hoped that 'it would comfort you in knowing that he fell in the Great Fight against Devilry'.[11] Such rhetoric rings hollow when set against the simple inscription on a plaque in St Mark's, Newtownards, to the two Cooke brothers killed in France in August and September 1916: 'our sons.' Another intimate tribute was provided when the Holywood sculptor, Rosamond Praeger, carved a bronze bas relief to the war dead from her Non-Subscribing Presbyterian congregation. The names included her brother, Egmont, who had served in the navy and died of diabetes in 1919

The ghosts of No Man's Land on the Mulholland stained glass window in Ballywalter Church of Ireland (1921) (Courtesy of Jane Leonard)

soon after his discharge.[12]

Some memorials were commissioned jointly by groups and individuals. An early example, unveiled in late 1915, was a stained glass window in St Comgall's Church of Ireland in Bangor. It commemorated Lieutenant Vivian Rea, a pre-war divinity student at Trinity College, Dublin. Designed by the Dublin studio, *An Túr Gloine* (the Tower of Glass), it portrayed a Christian knight and a harvest scene. The subscribers included family friends, Bangor scouts and his teachers and fellow students at Trinity.

School and club memorials

Throughout the war, prize day speeches stressed how many past pupils were on active service. At a function in Cottown Primary School

in February 1918, roll of honour with over fifty names was hung on the platform. After the war, many schools erected plaques. At Mourne Grange Preparatory School outside Kilkeel, a conventional war record of old boys was printed, but a more striking monument was the school's purchase of surplus huts from Ballykinlar for use as extra classrooms. These were re-named Victory Hall, Woolwich, Ypres, Marne and Somme. Individual memorials were also endowed by families, including the Wilson McBride Room at Rockport Preparatory School which remembered a past pupil killed in Italy in 1917.

Former members of scout troops, the Boys' Brigade and the Church Lads' Brigade were prompt to respond to the war, especially in Newry and Newtownards. When a local journalist queried in 1928 why such groups were included in Newry's Armistice Day ceremonies, he was advised to inspect the plaque in the local Scout Hall. Down Cathedral compiled a list of 29 former choristers on active service and erected a plaque to one, Sergeant William Love, who died of war related illness in 1919.

Sports clubs that compiled rolls of honour included Ards Hockey Club, Donaghadee Golf Club, Downpatrick Rifle Club and the Down Hunt. Many of their members were regular or reserve officers. By 1915, there were 27 on the Downpatrick Rifle Club's active service list. For decades after the war, printed membership lists for the Down Hunt were preceded by its roll of honour. In 1919 and 1920, Victory Cups were established by several golf clubs, and the Downpatrick Homing Pigeon Club staged a Victory Sweepstakes Race from Drogheda to Downpatrick to mark the Peace celebrations of July 1919.

Workplace memorials

Postal and railway officials were commemorated in their workplaces. Newry Post Office unveiled an illuminated war record in July 1916 which listed 25 staff. The cooperation of the local UVF and Irish Volunteers in guarding Newry Post Office during the Easter Rising was commended in speeches to mark the event. The Downpatrick Post Office followed Newry's example in 1920 when it unveiled a list of 20 staff including four killed. Guests at the ceremony included a female member of staff, Miss Gibson, who had served in France with the Telegraph Corps. The main memorial to the war service of 150 employees of the Belfast and County Down Railway, erected in 1922 at the Queen's Quay terminus in Belfast, included staff from its rural stations. County Down branch officials were also recorded in the printed war records of large institutions including many Irish banks and the Singer Sewing Machine Company (whose active service list issued at Christmas 1914 embraced its Bangor and Newtownards representatives).

Two attractive illuminated rolls of honour were commissioned by firms in Ballynahinch and Newtownards. The Drumaness Mills roll was printed by Bairds in Belfast. It recorded 23 men on active service, most of whom were in the RIR. The names were surmounted by a rich montage of the Allied flags below which were depictions of the mill and the theatres of war. This roll is now deposited in Down County Museum (see page 41). In June 1915, the Glen Printing and Finishing Company in Newtownards announced that 58 of its male workforce of 115 had joined up, many with the local 13th RIR. At a farewell party hosted by the firm's owner, a souvenir photograph was taken of his workers before they departed to France with the Ulster Division. The group included Captain Elliott Johnston, who had managed the hemsticking department. Johnston was killed on 1 July 1916.[13] By November 1917, when the firm unveiled an illuminated roll of honour (produced in-house), 91 employees had joined up of whom 12 had been killed.

An inventory of 'men employed in the Londonderry Collieries and Estates Serving in H.M. Army and Navy' contained 2,787 names, most of whom were colliery workers in England. Of 192 estate, office and steamer employees on active service, only five were from Mount Stewart. This figure seems oddly low (former employees serving against HM forces, such as German footmen on the pre-war staff of Mount Stewart, were naturally excluded).[14] More forceful evidence of the lingering significance of landed estates is provided by the Inch churchyard plaque

(described earlier, which includes many Finnebrogue workers) and by the congregrational memorials of Strean Presbyterian Church, Newtownards, and Ballygilbert Presbyterian Church. When unveiling the Strean stained glass windows in 1920, Lord Londonderry noted that all eight of those killed in the war had been born on his estate. At Ballygilbert Presbyterian Church, built on land donated by the Marquess of Dufferin and Ava, the memorial to the fallen lists Clandeboye estate workers along with gentry casualties, including the Anglican Lord Basil Blackwood (brother of the 2nd Marquess).[15]

Fraternal memorials

Of the many framed scrolls of honour produced by Orange lodges, the most extensive was that of Newtownards No 4 District which listed several hundred brethren on active service. Outdoor memorials were erected while the war was in progress. An arch erected over the main street in Banbridge in 1917 was inscribed: In Memoriam Ulster Division; Dinna Forget July 1st 1916.

Addressing Lecale Orangemen at the 12th July demonstration in 1917, Colonel James Craig, MP, correctly predicted that Thiepval would soon be emblazoned on Orange banners alongside Derry, Aughrim and the Boyne. The first lodge in Ireland to unfurl such a banner, reproducing James Beadle's painting of the Ulster Division's charge, was Stuart's Volunteers LOL 872 in Newtownards. Its banner was dedicated on 1 July 1918 on the same day that Beadle's original was presented to Belfast Corporation.[16] During the 1920s, the Somme battle featured on scores of Down banners. It is replicated on over a dozen still in use.[17]

While the Somme scene conjured up courage in battle, the reality of the war's losses was better conveyed on banners portraying the faces of those who died. Most memorial banners carried a single portrait of a local officer. The most sombre example of communal loss was that of Waringstown LOL 83. Unfurled in July 1920 by the widow of Major Holt Waring, it showed the solemn faces of her husband and eight others from his lodge who had died in the

Where are the lads of the village tonight? A sombre banner painted for Waringstown LOL 83 by Bridgett Brothers in 1920 (Courtesy of Jane Leonard)

war. In her speech, Mrs Waring hoped that wherever the lodge marched, it would live up to the ideal of duty as portrayed by the banner. Further reminders donated by Mrs Waring included a framed portrait of Major Holt Waring, and three drums also bearing his image. A banner still carried by a nearby Dollingstown lodge confirms that the memory of the war has not faded in rural Orangeism. It shows demobilised soldiers returning to their families on the village green, with the caption, 'every house mourned'.[18]

While banners provided a mobile memorial, many lodges also commissioned wall plaques. Seventeen out of 40 members of Kilmore Church Defenders LOL 237 served in the war and five were killed. The lodge unveiled a plaque in the local schoolhouse, near Moira, in 1921. Though the plaque has disappeared, the lodge still holds a 'dugout dinner' each November in memory of its war dead. The stone plaque in Downpatrick's Orange Hall to 22 fallen brethren, carved by the local Hastings firm, is rich in its iconography. King Billy rides his horse under the names of the fallen while a bugler of the RIR plays the *Last Post*. A Bible and Crown and furled regimental standards complete the tableau. The advertisement for the unveiling in 1920 invited survivors, next of kin and Protestant friends to attend.[19]

Masonic lodges were no less assiduous in commemorating their dead. Service records from 46 Down lodges were included in the *Grand Lodge of Free and Accepted Masons of Ireland Roll of Honour, 1914–1919* (Dublin, 1923), to which there was no Orange counterpart. Plaques were erected in masonic halls in Newry and Saintfield while in Comber, a memorial apron was presented to Masonic Lodge 46 by the widow of Captain George J Bruce, killed in October 1918 while serving with the Ulster Division.[20] Other war commemorations by fraternities in Down included a roll of honour produced in Newry by the Iveagh Yew Tree Lodge of the British Order of Ancient and Free Gardeners.

No memorials erected by nationalist fraternities in Down have so far been traced, although some endorsed war commemorations. In 1926, the AOH band accompanied its Orange counterpart in the Portaferry British Legion parade while in the late 1920s, the INF sold poppies in its Newry clubhouse. The St Joseph's Brass and Reed Band in Newry performed at concerts to raise funds for local war memorials.

Comrades' memorials

The principal tributes to County Down's service with the RIR are located in the towns where its militia battalions were based. In

DOWNPATRICK ORANGE HALL
War Memorial.

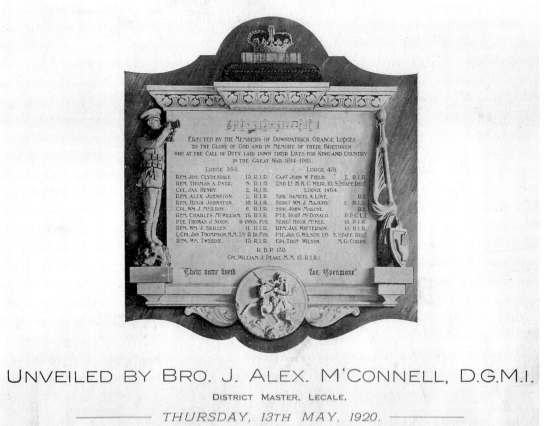

ERECTED BY THE MEMBERS OF DOWNPATRICK ORANGE LODGES
TO THE GLORY OF GOD AND IN MEMORY OF THEIR BRETHREN
WHO AT THE CALL OF DUTY LAID DOWN THEIR LIVES FOR KING AND COUNTRY
IN THE GREAT WAR, 1914-1919.

UNVEILED BY BRO. J. ALEX. M'CONNELL, D.G.M.I.
DISTRICT MASTER, LECALE.
THURSDAY, 13TH MAY, 1920.

The newspaper advertisement for the unveiling ceremony in Downpatrick Orange Hall rather unnecessarily made 'Protestant friends welcome' (DCM 1994–130)

Newtownards, a stained glass window in St Mark's Church of Ireland remembers the dead of the 4th RIR (North Downs). At Down Cathedral, a stained glass window to the fallen of the 5th RIR (South Downs) was dedicated in 1924. Its design, by the Scottish artist James Ballentine, aptly reflected the battalion's disembodied status, depicting a knight who had fought the good fight. In the same church, in November 1928, a plaque was unveiled to the 13th RIR. Special buses from Belfast, Banbridge and Bangor brought over 300 survivors in addition to many widows and war orphans. So packed was the congregation, that hundreds had to stand outside (see page 7). The other significant RIR monuments were to a commanding officer killed in France in 1917. Brother officers of the two reserve battalions that had been commanded by Colonel TVP McCammon erected plaques in Down Cathedral and in Holywood Church of Ireland in addition to unveiling a memorial portrait by William Conor in the officers' mess at Holywood. The plaques, carved by the Hastings firm, featured two riflemen in relief.[21]

In 1921, Bangor's veterans marked Armistice Week by unveiling three bronze plaques listing 116 local war fatalities. The memorial, designed by an architect, Capt AK Stewart, was commissioned by the local post of the Comrades of the Great War. A commemorative album with the photographs and service details of each man was displayed at the unveiling. While many had trained at nearby Clandeboye before active service with the 36th Division, the album also included some who had died with the 16th (Irish) Division. Subscriptions to the fund included the matinée takings at the Picture Palace, donated by the manager. By the time the plaques, featuring the CGW crest, were unveiled in the Abbey Street clubhouse, the CGW was no more, having merged with other ex-service organisations to form the British Legion (NI area). The album survives in the care of the North Down Heritage Centre.

The camaraderie of the Western Front also featured in the inter-war streetscapes of County Down via the ex-service housing schemes erected by the Irish Soldiers and Sailors Land Trust.

These included Arras Park in Bangor and Vimy Terrace in Newry. Local war heroes sometimes provided the inspiration for local authority housing also, as in De Wind Drive in Comber, built in 1961 in honour of Edmund de Wind, VC. Redburn Square in Holywood where the town memorial was unveiled in 1922 was so renamed after the family home of John Dunville, VC.

District memorials

Between 1921 and 1939, district memorials were erected in 19 towns and villages, mostly in north and mid Down. There are few in east and south Down. South of Killyleagh and Downpatrick, apart from Newcastle, there is none along the coast before Newry. Nor is any located on the Ards peninsula south of Newtownards and Ballywalter. The absence of a memorial variously reflected the dominance of nationalism, civic apathy or a committee's failure to agree on a design or location.

Most district memorials were erected during the first decade of peace. Ballynahinch and Newtownards were rather tardy (both 1934) while Newry's was not completed until 1939. Rathfriland's clock tower, planned from 1930, was not in place until after World War Two. Donaghcloney's memorial was inaugurated when convalescent soldiers donated money for the scheme during 1918. Holywood's plans were unveiled in July 1918, when a public meeting chaired by Sir James Craig was held in the Town Hall. A committee was elected. It reported that some £400 had already been collected and that a site near the railway station had been acquired. By August 1919, a design and sculptor (Leonard Merrifield, who also carved the Carson, Craigavon and Comber statues) had been agreed. Only £250 remained to be raised and the committee, anxious that the memorial be endorsed by the whole town, appealed for small donations from many rather than soliciting large cheques from a few. The unveiling was held in January 1922.

By comparison, Downpatrick's progress was leisurely. The cousin of Tommy Hastings, the main stonemason involved, has recalled that he spent much of the five years after the Armistice on the carving. A newspaper photograph of November 1923 showed Hastings painstakingly roughing out his sculpture. The result, a naïve and oddly proportioned rifleman in Portland stone, was unveiled in 1925. It was probably the most unsuccessful monument produced by the Church Street works and lacked the delicacy of his relief carvings on memorials elsewhere. The Downpatrick town clerk told his children that 'the memorial was so awful that when it was unveiled one old soldier in the crowd had dropped dead'.[22]

Towns awaiting permanent monuments often made do with War Office trophies as a focus for

WAR MEMORIAL AND STATION SQUARE, BALLYNAHINCH, CO.DOWN   R 2428

As elsewhere, the war memorial in Ballynahinch (1934) was near the hut where veterans socialised (DCM 1999–109)

58

Armistice Day ceremonies. Most trophies were German cannon taken on the Western Front, though Downpatrick's was a Russian piece commandeered by the 13th RIR. Bangor opted for a U19 submarine gun reflecting the town's pride in the Jutland exploits of the Honourable Edward Bingham, VC. Few towns refused such offers apart from Newry where the Board of Guardians and the Urban Council (both nationalist-controlled) declined to take 'a load of old scrap iron'. In Kilkeel, where no district memorial was erected, a German war gun continued to fill that role. In 1928, the Workhouse Guardians debated whether to scrap the gun (vandalised by local boys the previous Halloween). Worried that this would seem disrespectful to the memory of the part played 'by Mourne lads on the fields of Flanders', the Guardians voted to keep the gun.

Captured trophies might be used to shame the inactive. Veterans in Dromore marked the Somme anniversary in 1926 by dragging the German gun from the railway station to the square and placed a wreath on it 'in memory of the war memorial committee'. The Urban Council were sufficiently embarrassed to have the bronze rifleman in place by the following year.[23] Makeshift gestures were employed to less effect in Newtownards in the late 1920s, where veterans made a snowman soldier outside the Council offices, decorating him with war medals and a sign, 'Lest we forget'. Fined a shilling for loitering, the veterans did not get their permanent memorial until 1934.[24]

Once preliminary subscriptions were received, the main challenge for committees was to ensure that all qualifying names were included. Draft lists were circulated. Usually this was done via newspapers and churches though, in Comber, the draft was posted in the window of James Niblock's hardware shop, requesting alterations and additions to be handed in there. Completed memorials also featured in shop windows. On Armistice Day in Killyleagh in 1928, Jay Faulkiner's stationery shop displayed a model of the Unknown Soldier's monument in his window, accompanied by poppies, flags, wreaths and images of wooden crosses. To raise funds for the Kilbroney parish sale of work in 1926, Miss Armstrong's chemist's shop in Rostrevor sold photographs of the church war memorial and printed copies of the active service list.

The task of gathering names was easier in towns where the wartime press had featured service lists. The *Newtownards Chronicle* published a comprehensive street by street sequence between July and October 1915. Trade directories like the *Newtownards Almanac*, whose 1917 edition included the photographs and details of local fatalities, also documented the war's impact. When Newtownards finally unveiled a memorial in 1934, the *Chronicle* published its wartime lists in a souvenir booklet.

Once names were gathered, the dilemmas about inclusion and the ordering of names had to be tackled. Almost all district memorials were dedicated to the fallen, though some also listed survivors on rear and side panels. Groomsport differed in distinguishing between foreign and home service (and also by including merchant seamen) while Gilford arranged names by townland of origin, thus greatly aiding future genealogists.

Committees usually composed local gentry (who often donated sites), ex-officers, businessmen, Protestant clergy and unionist politicians. Nationalist and Catholic membership was rare. In Newtownards, the parish priest attended a meeting to plan a memorial in 1919, but thereafter Catholic representation ceased. No Catholic priest took part in Armistice Day or Remembrance Sunday ceremonies at the Downpatrick monument until 1966. Unveiling speeches throughout Down equated war service with the 36th (Ulster) Division, thus excluding the contribution of nationalists. Addressing the crowd at Ballywalter's unveiling in 1922, the GOC for Northern Ireland described the Ulster Division as a typical new army formation in uniting citizens of all classes, professions and trades. Creeds were not mentioned. It is not surprising that few nationalist councillors attended Armistice Day ceremonies throughout Down during this period.[25] Nationalist reactions to Newry's memorial are discussed at the end of this article.

WAR MEMORIAL, BALLYWALTER

R 3048

PG Bantham's rifleman (1922) on guard where village and harbour meet in Ballywalter (DCM 1999-113)

Few women apart from gentry widows sat on memorial committees. Killyleagh was exceptional in that its memorial was inaugurated by the Killyleagh Women's Guild. Though the committee expanded to include men, the women kept control of the funds and the cheque for the completed plaque, £123 15s, was signed by Mrs Young, the secretary. The formidable Mrs Waring dominated memorial projects in her area, advising on designs and scrutinising names for inclusion. She unveiled the Waringstown clocktower and about a dozen other memorials in churches, Orange halls and adjoining villages. Occasionally, the mothers of soldiers were allowed ceremonial duties. The Holywood memorial was unveiled by Mrs Dunlop, the mother of the first soldier to die, while the wreath laid on behalf of the townspeople was placed by Mrs Elliott, Sullivan Street, mother of three sons killed in the war.[26]

Squares, parks and crossroads were the most favoured sites for memorials. Ards villages like Groomsport, Donagahadee and Ballywalter placed their tributes close to the sea. The Castlewellan and Killyleagh plaques were mounted on the walls of prominent buildings. Downpatrick's statue (originally intended to be in front of the courthouse) was sited next to the cricket ground. Though not in the town centre, this was at the junction of two major roads.

Some committees agonised for years over possible designs. Ballywalter juggled the relative artistic merits and costs of a clock tower, an obelisk, a celtic cross and a bugler before opting for a statue of a rifleman at arms. In Bangor, the committee considered erecting a district nurses' hostel, swimming or saltwater baths, a clubhouse and a pier before deciding on an obelisk in Ward Park, dedicated in 1927. In Newtownards, the numerous options included various schools, a fire station and a maternity hospital (as well as many of the ideas suggested in Bangor). One of the most attractive and unusual schemes proposed for Newtownards was a Victory Avenue planted with trees associated with Northern France and Belgium, yet the outcome was another dreary obelisk.

The most unusual sculpture was the crouching lion by Francis Wiles, the Lame sculptor, completed for Newcastle promenade in 1927. Seven districts chose statues of riflemen or buglers. In Banbridge, Frederick Pomeroy's celebrating infantryman towered over the town. The base panels featured dramatic friezes of four turning points in the war, from Le Cateau in August 1914 to the Armistice. Other popular designs included obelisks (6) and wall plaques (3). Figurative sculpture was predominantly male, with female Victory figures featuring only on the Bangor and Newtownards obelisks. The only specifically Irish design was the celtic cross erected at Hillsborough, where Lord Arthur Hill

FRANCIS WILES
SCULPTOR

F. EARL ANNESLEY
F. BURNS
H. COOPER
A DIGGES-LA-TOUCHE
E DIGGES-LA-TOUCHE
D. EWING
J. GEDDES
J. GREER
J.V. KNOX
V. LAW
A. MALCOLMSON
G.W. MATTHEWS

D. LAWSON   W.J. PORTER
M.F. McHENRY   H.W. PORTER
J. McDOWELL   W. CRORY
H. MAGEE   J.P. HYLAND

Originally erected on the promenade, Francis Wiles' crouching lion in Newcastle (1927) may be on the move again, according to press reports during 2004

provided his own drawings and had to be dissuaded by the stonemasons from including snakes (rarely found on Irish crosses!).

Commemoration was profitable. From 1916 onwards, orders passed into firms like Hastings in Downpatrick, Emerson in Banbridge and Purdy and Millard in Belfast. Over fifty men were employed at Newcastle in March 1920 quarrying granite for war memorials. While some committees favoured designs from eminent sculptors and stained glass artists from London, Dublin, Belfast and Edinburgh, all expressed great pride in using local materials. The Newtownards obelisk, quarried from Mourne granite in Newry, was declared to be 'in reality a County Down memorial for County Down men.' The Revd Andrew Gibson, dedicating the Waringstown clock tower with its distinctive facing in local whinstone, considered that the collaboration of a Belfast clock maker, a Lurgan builder and a Banbridge architect enhanced its beauty all the more. Castlewellan's polished

granite plaque, mounted on the outside wall of the courthouse, had particularly local associations. It was donated by Lady Mabel Annesley in memory of her brother Francis, the 6th Earl, killed with the Royal Flying Corps in 1914. The slab had been given to her father when the Castlewellan quarries won the contract for the Albert Memorial steps in London.

Conclusion

The history of Down's war memorials after 1939 falls outside the scope of this article. The dilemmas and propriety of adding names from conflicts other than World War Two are just two aspects.[27] However, the torturous story of the Newry memorial, erected in 1939, provides a salutary example of what was to follow. A decision in August 1938 by the Urban Council, to allow the British Legion to erect a cenotaph, was followed in October by similar permission for the Newry Old IRA Remembrance Association to erect a celtic cross to the dead of 1916–1923. While both applications were debated vigorously, most councillors supported the principle of equivalence and agreed with the chairman that it was time to acknowledge all aspects of Newry's past. Two weeks later, the Northern Ireland government prohibited the IRA memorial. The Legion was forced to cancel its Armistice Day church service 'in deference to the feelings of the vast majority of the people of the town', who were outraged at the banning of the IRA memorial. It seemed impossible to reconcile opinion in the town, with republicans demanding that no memorial to the Great War be proceeded with, while veterans insisted that their cenotaph should not be sacrificed because of the government's action. The cenotaph was quietly completed the following summer. No ceremony of dedication was held and the names of the war dead were not inscribed for fear that lingering resentment might be expressed in defacement. In 1994, the cenotaph was finally dedicated, and in 2002, a comprehensive biographical register of the town's war dead was published by the Equality Unit of Newry and Mourne District Council. This initiative was strongly endorsed by all political parties. However, the book's introduction omits the 1938 controversy and instead attributes the subsequent decision not to include names on the cenotaph 'to the cost involved, and the embarrassment, if after the names were engraved, it was found that someone had been overlooked.[28] Such constructions confirm how the divisions of inter-war Northern Ireland can still impinge on and inhibit current commemoration.

Jane Leonard is an historian at the Ulster Museum, Belfast, where she works with community groups on projects that explore the legacies of conflict in twentieth century Ireland. She curated the remembrance section of the museum's current exhibition, *Conflict*. She is currently writing an illustrated history of war commemoration in twentieth century Ireland and a study of the post-war lives of Irish veterans of the Great War.

Notes and References

1. A lively commemoration of the County Down home front survives in William Conor's portraits of officers and troops at Ballykinlar, Newcastle and Newtownards. The majority of these are deposited in the Ulster Museum and the Ulster Folk and Transport Museum while others are in the Royal Ulster Rifles Museum and in Down County Museum. Some officers who sat for Conor later died in the war and their next of kin then commissioned additional memorial portraits. The author is currently researching Conor's war art and would welcome information about portraits still in private possession.

2. All examples are taken from the author's database of Irish war memorials. Full citations will be included when this database, compiled from newspapers and periodicals, private and official archives, local histories and photographs, is published in gazeteer form. The author would welcome additional details on memorials in Down, especially in categories that appear to be under-represented. Newspapers used in researching this article included the *Banbridge Chronicle*, the *County Down Spectator*, the *Down Recorder*, the *Newtownards Chronicle*, the *Newry Reporter* – and the *Frontier Sentinel*. Researchers are also advised to consult the National Inventory of War Memorials, based at the Imperial War Museum, London. This currently includes 134 examples from County Down (chiefly in towns, villages and churches), but does not record individual names. This inventory is scheduled to go on-line in 2005.

3. This roll was an invaluable source for Colin Moffett (ed), *Newry's War Dead, 1914–1918, 1939–45*, Newry and Mourne District Council, 2002.

4. It is now displayed in the Council offices.

5. Andrew Doloughan, *Our Great Inheritance*, volume 1, pp 48-51.

6. See J & E McConaghy, *A Light For the Road*, (Belfast, 1991), p 73.

7. Keith Jeffery, *Ireland and the Great War* – (Cambridge, 2000), p 132 and his article, 'The Great War in Modern Irish Memory', in TG Fraser and Keith Jeffery (eds), *Men, Women and War* (Dublin, 1993), p 150; likewise Nuala C Johnson, *Ireland and the Great War and the Geography of Remembrance* (Cambridge, 2003), p 107.

8. Interview with the late Mary Woods, Seahornan, Ardglass, 1987, in which she recalled that such lists were read at wartime Masses in Dunsford and Ardglass.

9. Public Record Office of Northern Ireland, D3524/2/1 *Killyleagh Women's War Work & Patriotic Effort & Roll of Honour* (1918).

10. Of 254 military and naval World War One graves in County Down, 21 are located in Catholic cemeteries: see *The War Graves of the British Empire: Northern Ireland Register*, Imperial War Graves Commission (London, 1931), pp 51–65; the Keenan details are recorded in RJ Clarke, *Old Families of Downpatrick*.

11. Correspondence in Down County Museum.

12. Catherine Gaynor, 'An Ulster Sculptor, Sophia Rosamund Praeger (1867–1954)', *Irish Arts Review 2000*, p 41.

13. The group photograph is reproduced (but not dated) in Keith Haines, *North Down Memories. Photographs, 1860s–1960s* (Belfast, 2000), p 91.

14. Durham Record Office, Londonderry Estate Papers, *Roll of Honour*. One Newtownards veteran, interviewed by this author in August 1987, recalled meeting a captured German POW in late 1914, whose County Down accent resulted from his years as a footman at Mount Stewart.

15. Gentry sometimes featured on several district memorials (Lord Annesley is on the Castlewellan and Newcastle monuments) but seldom received different denominational tributes.

16. The Newtownards banner predates by a year the unfurling of a Somme banner by a Belfast lodge (Hydepark 1067), asserted by Neil Jarman, *Material Conflicts. Parades and Vivual Displays in Northern*

Ireland (Oxford, 1997), p 72, to be the first time that the Somme and the Boyne had been so connected.

17. Gable versions of Beadle's painting were painted post-war in Bangor and Newtownards. A present-day mural based on Beadle can be seen in the TA camp at Movilla.

18. One memoir of Dollingstown in the 1920s observed that 'almost the entire male population of the small village was obliterated' in the war, see Frank Pantridge, *An Unquiet Life* (privately printed, 1989), p 2; the Dollingstown banner, painted in 2000, was displayed in an exhibition on Orange military history at Schomberg House, Belfast, July 2004. I am grateful to Waringstown LOL 83 for permission to photograph its banner, and to David Scott, Grand Orange Lodge of Ireland, for his assistance in tracing other memorials.

19. I am grateful to Alex McShane for details on the dugout dinner. One of those listed on the Downpatrick plaque, William James Skillen, was not added to the town's memorial until 2001.

20. This apron is now in the Somme Heritage Centre, Conlig.

21. McCammon's portrait also featured on the banner of Holywood LOL 1687 which had been named McCammon's True Blues in 1905. 1 am grateful to David Fitzpatrick for clarifying the nomenclature and history of this lodge, and also for his comments on drafts of this article.

22. Dick Gifford, 'Downpatrick war memorial', *Lecale Miscellany*, 1993, pp 31–33; Maurice Hayes, *Black Pudding And Slim. A Downpatrick Boyhood* (Belfast, 1996), p 166.

23. Dromore's problems did not end with the unveiling. The war memorial committee's deficit was eventually written off by a local bank. I am grateful to Drew Nelson for this reference.

24. This snowman was recently commemorated in a poetic salute to those who 'couldn't wait to remember; see Michael Longley, 'The Cenotaph', in *The Weather in Japan*, (London, 2000), p 20.

25. For the cease-fires' impact on nationalist attitudes to war commemoration, see my article, 'The Twinge of Memory: Armistice Day and Remembrance Sunday in Dublin since 1919' in Richard English and Graham Walker (eds) *Unionism in Modern Ireland* (London, 1996), pp 99–114, and also my reviews of *Newry's War Dead* in *Familia*, 2003 and Alex Maskey's Somme initiative in *Fortnight*, June 2003.

26. For further detail on the Holywood memorial, see the *County Down Spectator*, 17 November 1995.

27. These include lengthy campaigns to add UDR and RUC fatalities from the Troubles to district war memorials, and council plaques erected in recent years on the Ards and elsewhere to the dead of the two world wars and subsequent conflicts; see my articles cited above and also my pamphlet, *Memorials to the Casualties of Conflict: Northern Ireland, 1969–97* (Belfast, 1997)

28. See Moffett, *op cit*, pX.

Newry's War Dead

Colin Moffet

Located on Ireland's east coast between Belfast and Dublin, Newry has played an influential role in Ireland's social, cultural and political development. Adding to this knowledge, Newry and Mourne District Council's publication *Newry's War Dead* was launched by the highly acclaimed military historian Professor Keith Jeffery, of the University of Ulster, in Newry Arts Centre on the evening of Tuesday 12 November 2002. The book is the result of research by the Community Relations Section of the Council's Equality Unit, and details those from the Newry area who gave their lives in the two World Wars.

When Newry's War Memorial was first erected in 1938 it had been decided not to inscribe the names of those who had been killed or served in the war because of the cost involved and the embarrassment, if after the names were engraved, it was found that someone had been overlooked. It was during 1999, that Newry and Mourne District Council embarked on a project to officially record these names and it was envisaged they would be inscribed on the War Memorial situated at Bank Parade, Newry.

The research entailed various methods of data collection; Newry Royal British Legion was contacted, local churches provided the names on their Rolls of Honour, regular advertisements were placed in the press, the Commonwealth War Graves Commission supplied information of records on people with a Newry connection, and microfilm of newspapers from the time was

Newry's War Memorial, first erected at Trevor Hill in 1938, and later re-located to Bank Parade (Courtesy of Newry and Mourne Museum)

analysed. An integral part of the process was the public consultation, during which the information was placed on display at eleven locations across the Newry City area, and afforded the community an opportunity to view, amend and provide additional names.

It was at this stage that the enormity of the whole project began to emerge. The fact that there were so many names, added a new dimension and presented further challenges. Was there enough space on the memorial to inscribe the names? How should the list be treated – were the names to be inscribed as one set or should they be divided into two groups representing the First World War and Second World War? Was inscribing the names directly onto the War Memorial the most viable and suitable solution?

Reflecting upon the original decision in 1938 not to inscribe the names for fear of overlooking someone, it was recognised that this was not the definitive list, and space would have to be left on the memorial for names to be added in the future. This presented a further logistical problem wherein additional names would then be out of alphabetical sequence and future generations may view them as being listed in order of importance.

It was agreed that the best way to proceed was to print a book containing the names of those who gave their lives in the two World Wars, and in addition produce a loose-leaf memorial book. The loose-leaf book has been produced and will provide an invaluable historical resource for future local research. As a piece of living history, accessible for reference in Newry Museum, the loose-leaf memorial book with one name per page has the advantage and flexibility of allowing further names to be inserted.

Newry's War Dead lists the names of 373 individuals from the Newry area who lost their lives in the two World Wars, and beside each name we have recorded the individual's regiment and rank, date of death, cemetery, panel number and grave reference, and additional information such as their home address. We are indebted to all those who shared their memories, stories and information, and are grateful especially to those who provided memorabilia such as photographs and letters to illustrate the book

As you read *Newry's War Dead* you will gain a sense of Newry's influence and past glory as a major port, wherein one in every five of those who lost their lives were Merchant Seamen or members of the Royal Navy. This makes the book unique and quite distinct from many other lists of war dead.

Cyril Wiltshire, Lance Corporal 1/5th Battalion, Welsh Regiment, whose diary entries and letters are included in the book (Courtesy of Bria Heron)

While the list of names is a testament and solemn memorial to the men and women who lost their lives, it must be remembered that behind each name is an individual or family who suffered bereavement and had to deal with the consequences of their loss.

Reflecting upon areas of service and the differing levels of impact this loss had upon the family unit, the appendices have eight themes – the soldier, the seaman, the airman, the son, the family, the neighbourhood, the village of Bessbrook, and extracts from local papers. Describing personal experiences such as the words of the soldier, Cyril Wiltshire, from his last diary entry, and reflecting the struggle of seaman Bernard Golding's widow, Mary, to obtain a pension for the loss of her husband, these appendices provide a rich source of learning. These were not just men and women, they were fathers, mothers, sons, daughters, grandfathers, grandmothers, aunts and uncles. Every family has a unique (and tragic) story to tell and we have chosen some examples to illustrate the personal and human side of this loss.

Newry's War Dead formally acknowledges the Newry area's Unknown Soldiers – those who for our today gave their tomorrow. This is an essential part of the process to collectively recognise and remember those who died, and the book should prove to be a valuable historical resource for everyone. It is not simply a list of names, and the human stories leave a lasting impression and underline the impact of this loss on the families and our community left behind.

Human stories contained within the appendices record the impact of the two World Wars upon the local area. Every family has a unique and tragic story to tell, and it is important to help the wider community recognize that those who died were not all career soldiers.

Indeed, the people who lost their lives were valued members of our community. This is clearly illustrated in the following report of the ceremony for the presentation of Newry's Roll of Honour on 28 April 1915, which incorporates and celebrates a sense of unity and the rich cultural and international diversity among the citizens of Newry at that time.

Frontier Sentinel. Saturday, May 1, 1915
'NEWRY'S ROLL OF HONOUR
REMARKABLE DEMONSTRATION
ALL CREEDS AND CLASSES FRATERNISE

A meeting of unexampled dimensions, cordiality and enthusiasm took place in the Town Hall, Newry, on Wednesday night, the occasion being the presentation to the Chairman of the Urban Council (Mr Hugh J McConville, J.P.), on behalf of the town, of Newry's Roll of Honour in the present European War. The entertainment was a most enjoyable one, most of those present being relatives and friends of those whose names appear on the roll. Every creed and class was represented, and the function was an indescribably inspiring one. All the local bands, Nationalist and Unionist, were present, and paraded the town before and after the proceedings.

The proceedings opened with a popular selection of musical items by the St Joseph's Brass and Reed Band (under the conductorship of Mr Terence Ruddy), after which the Rev Father Timmerman, a Belgian refugee priest, supported by a party of refugees, sang the Belgium National Anthem. The anthem was illustrated by views of King George V and of King Albert reviewing the Belgium troops in Belgium. Master William Johnson (son of Mr William Johnson, solicitor) next sang 'Tipperary', the chorus being joined in by the 1st Newry (Earl of Kilmorey's) troop of Boy Scouts. In connection with this song a picture showing how Michael O'Leary won the Victoria Cross was exhibited. Mr P. J. Boden sang in French 'The Marseillaise' with suitable pictorial representation. This was followed by 'The Minstrel Boy,' which was rendered by Mr Walter Alderdice, after which 'God Save the King' was sung by a male choir. The Victoria Fife and Drum Band then played an appropriate selection and this was followed by a cinematograph picture.

The Rev Father Timmerman, who briefly addressed the vast meeting, received a cordial and hearty welcome. He said he had been three months now in Ireland, and he was obliged to return to Belgium, but he could not leave Ireland without thanking them all for their kindness to them (the refugees). *(Applause)* He hoped they would continue that kindness to those of them that remained, and that they would soon – very soon – be able to return to Belgium. He hoped their country would be clear of all the Germans after the great battle on the Year. *(Loud applause)*

The formal presentation of the roll of honour afterwards took place. The roll contains 867 names, and the beautifully illuminated cover bears, in addition to the flags of the Allies and the Arms of Newry, the following inscription: 'European War, 1914 – Newry roll of honour, being a list of names of men serving in his Majesty's army and navy since the outbreak of the war. Presented to Mr H. J. McConville, Esq., J.P., chairman of the Newry Urban Council, on behalf of the town, at a public meeting held in the Town Hall, Newry, on the 28th April, 1915.'

On the motion of Mr Kerr, seconded by Mr

O'Rorke, the chair was taken, amid applause, by Mr H. J. McConville, J.P., who called upon the town clerk to read the apologies for non-attendance. These included a telegram from Mr J. J. Mooney M.P., stating that it had been his intention to be present that evening in order that, as member for the borough, he might join in emphasising the unity which existed and the desire of all parties to do their duty to King and country in the present crisis. He regretted, however, that the alteration in the business of the House prevented his attendance, but he would like to join in paying any tribute that he could to the brave men who had already gone from Frontier Town, and who, he well knew, would worthily uphold the name and traditions of their ancient town.

Mr Thomas P. Willis, vice-chairman of the Urban Council, said that it was his privilege to present to the chairman Newry's roll of honour on behalf of that ancient borough. In honouring their brave soldiers and sailors Newry men honoured and elevated themselves. They were proud of their gallant soldiers and sailors and wished gratefully to acknowledge their heroic services. *(Applause)* What was the prime object of that meeting? The answer was, 'It is to promote and encourage the patriotic spirit now prevailing.' What magnetic power was it that that had brought together from north and south, east and the west, and the lands beyond the seas, the magnificent and powerful British Army? One little word of four letters – 'duty.' *(Applause)* What an inspiration. The Allies, soldiers and sailors, were doing their duty, sealing it with their blood. Let those who were obliged to stay at home do their duty. In conclusion, he formally handed over the roll of honour, amidst intense enthusiasm.

Rev Father F. J. O'Hare, C.C., delivered a stirring speech, in the course of which he said that they were all deeply indebted to those sailors and soldiers who formed and were forming the ring of fire that guards our lives and liberties. (Applause) It was indeed no figure of speech to assert that they were their (the soldiers' and sailors') debtors. It was also satisfactory to know that the Frontier Town had won its title to some geographical prominence, and that it had sent to the colours a larger proportion of its sons than any other town in

Ireland. They heard little now, and they would hear less in the future, of the decline of the martial spirit in Ireland and of the dearth of recruits in this country. *(Applause)* They could not all, as had been said, join the colours or take their place in the fighting line; but they could all do some service at home, as 'they also served who only watch – and wait.' It was that sense that they made the presentation of that Roll of Honour of Newry's sons that night. *(Loud applause)*

Rev H. B. Swanzy, M.A., Vicar of St. Mary's, said there was little need for him to add anything to what had been so eloquently said to them by Father O'Hare, but as a native of that town of Newry he could not come there amongst the people of Newry and hear the references to that roll without saying in the name of the people of Newry how proud they all were that it held the premier place in the whole of Ireland for the number of its sons, in proportion to their numbers, who had gone out to face the foe. *(Applause)* They remembered the poster that was put up on many of their walls of one soldier lying wounded, and of another standing up before the battle line and looking back to his own country and saying 'Will they never come?' They were proud of the 900 men who were doing so well, but let everyone else who had the power give himself to his country now. *(Applause)*

The Rev W. G. Strahan, B.A., minister of Sandys Street Presbyterian Church, said he felt very proud indeed when asked to say a few words at that meeting that night, as it was indeed a truly patriotic meeting composed of all creeds and classes. The men who had gone out from Newry to fight had gone out to fight for their King and country, and for the liberties that belonged to our Empire. Newry in some respects, it might be said, was a retrograde town, but in regard to the present war she had taken the lead, and had sent forth a proportion of her citizens that no other town in proportion to her population could boast of. *(Applause)*

The Chairman in accepting the roll of honour on behalf of the town, gratefully acknowledged the spirit which brought about the presentation, and promised that the document would be treasured as one of the most interesting records in the annals of Newry.

Mr Alex Fisher proposed a vote of thanks to the Belgians, the band, the Boy Scouts, the vocalists, Mr Wm. Johnson, the accompanist and to the town clerk (who prepared the roll of honour, with the assistance of members of the R.I.C.)

The motion was put to the meeting, and passed with enthusiasm, the chairman adding the name of Mr Fisher, to whom, he said, they owed a great deal for all the time and trouble he had devoted to the movement which had resulted in the presentation of the Roll of Honour.

The St Patrick's Flute Band, under the conductorship of Mr John Reilly, then rendered a pleasing selection, and this was followed by a specially selected war drama, 'The Dear Little Shamrock,' illustrated by suitable slides, was sung by Mr Boden. Mr Jack Blair was next heard with pleasure in 'Land of Hope and Glory,' and after the Russian National Anthem had been rendered, the entertainment was brought to a close by the playing of 'A Nation Once Again' by St Joseph's Band and 'God Save the King,' the audience all rising to their feet while the last mentioned item was being discoursed.

Mr William Johnson, solicitor, rendered the accompaniments during the evening in a highly satisfactory manner.'

The launch of *Newry's War Dead* in November 2002 was a truly cross-community event. All sections of the community, and indeed every political party was represented. Furthermore, the project has had other dimensions.

In 2002, during the research process, the Council ran a schools project in conjunction with the Southern Education and Library Board. Five post primary schools across the Newry and Mourne area participated in the project, which allowed students to develop their research and data analysis skills through learning about the local historical context of the two World Wars.

In addition, since the launch of the book, the Northern Ireland ad hoc 'Book of Honour' Committee, chaired by Sir Kenneth Bloomfield, has used *Newry's War Dead* as an example for how other District Councils could produce books to remember the sacrifice made by local people in their area.

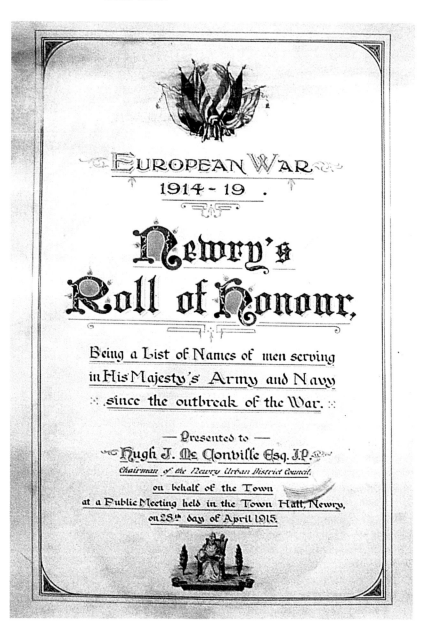

The cover of the Roll of Honour presented to the chairman of Newry Urban Council on 28 April 1915 (Courtsey of Mr L Taylor)

It is important to reflect that this project was not designed to be a history or museum project. This was an initiative that was an integral part of the Council's Community Relations programme to create greater awareness and understanding within the community. Within Northern Irish society we constantly identify and highlight difference between our communities, but it is always important to take time to revisit and identify our past shared history. This book is a fitting tribute to collectively recognize and remember all those who gave so much.

Priced at £5.00 (+ p&p), *Newry's War Dead* can be obtained from Colin Moffett, Equality Officer, Newry and Mourne District Council by phone (028) 3031 3081, or email email:Colin.Moffett@newryandmourne.gov.uk. Alternatively, you may purchase a copy by writing to Colin Moffett, Equality Officer, Newry and Mourne District Council, Council Offices, Monaghan Row, Newry, Co Down BT35 8DJ.

The editor of *Newry's War Dead*, Colin Moffett, of Newry & Mourne District Council's Equality Unit, is a first class honours graduate in History and Politics from the University of Ulster. He received the Thompson Memorial History Award in 1999.

From County Down to Anzac Cove: The tragic Great War journey made by a local soldier in the 10th (Irish) Division

Philip Orr

In 1914, when The Great War broke out, the building which now constitutes Down County Museum and which once began as a prison, was in fact playing the role of a military barracks. When Thomas Deddis from Hillsborough, in the north of the county, came to Downpatrick to enlist in the early days of that war, he walked through the gateway of the barracks, seeking to become a volunteer soldier in Kitcheners' New Army, made up of enthusiastic civilians. He could not have foreseen the journey which he would make as a member of the 10th (Irish) Division, sailing across The Mediteranean Sea to the Gallipoli Peninsula, as part of Winston Churchill's great plan to beat the Turkish Empire and bypass the quagmire of the Western Front.

Thomas Deddis was one of over a thousand men from Antrim and Down who joined the forces in these early days of the war, before the more famous 36th and 16th Divisions had been established. The 10th Division contained men from every regional infantry regiment in Ireland, as well as hundreds of men from across the Irish Sea. They trained at a number of camps, including the Curragh in County Kildare. Throughout the autumn and winter of 1914, they learned how to drill, to march, and to obey orders. Deddis's battalion commander was Colonel Eastwood from Dundalk. The overall commander of the 16,000 men in the complete division was General Sir Bryan Mahon, an Anglo-Irish military hero who had led the British forces which had relieved Mafeking during the Boer War.

After Christmas, the Division moved to Dublin for further training, which was a popular move, as men such as Thomas Deddis could enjoy several hours' leave each week in the busy capital, enjoying the expenditure of their army pay on bacon and eggs at a nearby café or a couple of glasses of beer in a local pub. Then, in April 1915 came the word that the Irish troops must move to Basingstoke in the south of England for further preparation before departure. Deddis must have been proud to march through the crowded streets of Dublin, en route for the docks. Flags of St Patrick fluttered from lamp posts and women in the crowd proffered chocolates, fruit and whisky to the soldiers as they passed by. Then, on a dark, damp night, the troopships left the Alexandra Basin and undertook a zigzag voyage across the Irish Sea, to avoid the attention of German U-boats.

It is hard to say whether a young volunteer soldier from County Down would have left Irish shores before, but in all probability it would have been a new experience for him to step ashore at Holyhead, in Wales, and then to take a long train-ride to Hampshire. Once there, he set up camp until July, focusing on learning the crucial skills of the army marksman with his Lee Enfield rifle, and the newly sought skills of the machine-gunner, whose weapon was so deadly and efficient.

By now the Irish soldiers were becoming more aware of the plan being made to send them to 'The East'. News was already breaking of the costly campaign being waged on the Gallipoli Peninsula, in which numerous Australasian troops had been deployed. Already, Irish veterans of the regular army had been ordered to storm the beaches at the southern tip of the Turkish headland, only to die when tangled in the barbed wire that lay beneath the water and to be shot to pieces by the enemy, who were safely positioned onshore.

In July 1915, Thomas and his fellow-soldiers were sent to Liverpool to board the famous liner the *Mauretania*, which had been converted for use as a troopship. This vessel had won the coveted 'Blue Riband' prize for the fastest ever crossing of

Soldiers preparing to leave the Royal Barracks, Dublin, destined for Gallipoli (Courtesy of Michael Lee, Dunlaoghaire)

the Atlantic, and the men must have been astounded by the ship's elegance and prowess, as well as somewhat nervous, given that the *Mauretania*'s sister-ship the *Lusitania*, had recently been sunk by a German U-boat attack.

The troopship sailed safely through the Irish Sea, across the Bay of Biscay and into the Mediterranean. The troops were heading for the Greek island of Lemnos, where the armies of Britain and France were based, within a short distance of the Gallipoli coastline. Plans were afoot for a new assault in a northern portion of the peninsula at a wide inlet called Suvla Bay. The 10th (Irish) Division would be heavily involved in this task of landing in the sandy bay at Cape Suvla, but a certain number of troops would be sent to Anzac Cove, a few miles to the south, in order to help the Australian and New Zealand soldiers who were busy struggling to move inland, in a coastal landscape dominated by steep cliffs, precipitous gullies and tenacious Turkish defence.

During the first week of August, the battalion which included Thomas Deddis set sail on small boats for a night-time journey to the Cove. It was a dark but cloudless summer night and the stars shone overhead. A few hours later, they could see the flash of the shellfire and hear the boom of the

guns from the headland, which was appearing in silhouette on the horizon. Under cover of darkness, the Irish soldiers approached the shoreline and transferred to the motorised 'lighters' which would transfer them the final yards to the beach. Successfully and safely, the 10th Division landed and within a couple of days they were preparing to engage in battle with the Turks, who occupied the heights above the exposed strand where the famous Anzac soldiers strode about, tending to their stores or the needs of the wounded. This was Thomas Deddis' first experience of a battlefield and it must have been terrifying, as at no time on the Gallipoli Peninsula could one ever count oneself out of harm's way.

The battalion to which Deddis belonged was given the task of participating in a fresh attack on the prominent hill known as the Chunuk Bair, where the new and gifted Turkish commander, Mustapha Kemal, was based. Already Deddis would have been aware not just of the dangers posed by gunfire and shells but of the crippling heat, the lack of regular water supplies and the terrible food, characterised by the 'bully beef' which had not 'travelled well' in the Mediterranean heat, and therefore poured out of the tin in a sticky and unpalatable mess.

Sadly, what lay ahead for Deddis' battalion was one of the most ghastly and swift massacres of the 10th Division's Gallipoli campaign. The battalion was faced with a hail of bullets from the heights above them. The slopes of the Chunuk Bair were bare, unprotected and, in places, incredibly steep and rocky. The Irishmen were picked off with incredible ease by the enemy, and those who were wounded were left lying on a sun-parched landscape in inaccessible places where stretcher-bearers could scarcely manage to reach them. During the first morning of their attack on the ridge, 800 men in the battalion– the majority of them from Antrim and Down – stepped out to do battle. Of those, 500 or more were killed, captured or wounded and the young officers in the battalion were virtually wiped out, including Colonel Eastwood, whose body was buried in a makeshift grave facing the sea.

Thomas Deddis was one of the lucky survivors of this massacre but his emotions must have been deeply disturbed by the ordeal. Within a couple of days the battalion was ordered into 'rest' mode and thereafter played little part in any further serious military action on the peninsula. However the scrub-covered landscape was littered with the dead, and the stink of corpses was accompanied by a swarm of flies, which feasted on the dead.

Water supplies and food became infected and gastric illnesses such as dysentery began to spread like wildfire through the British troops. The only consolation was the occasional letter from home and the fact that the Gallipoli Peninsula was in fact a startlingly beautiful place. Deddis was no doubt one of those soldiers who, at night, throughout the months of August and September, would take the chance to swim in the waters of the Mediterranean during the relative safety of the night-hours. If the young County Down soldier had had any classical education or any knowledge of history, he would have realised that just a few miles to the south-east lay the Asian shoreline and the site of the famous battle of Troy.

In late September, the decision was taken to evacuate the Irish troops from Gallipoli. The main part of the Division had landed at Suvla Bay as planned back in early August, but the anticipated breakthrough had not occurred and many thousands of men had either been injured or had lost their lives, many in horrible circumstances. The tinder-dry scrub had been set on fire due to the intensity of the British bombardment and, as a result, many men had been burned alive whilst awaiting rescue by stretcher-bearers on the Suvla hillslopes. The soldiers who now lined up to be evacuated from Gallipoli included many men

Anzac Cove, Gallipoli (Courtesy of Brian Wilson)

whose nightmares were full of the terrible things which they had witnessed and who would, in post-war years, be labelled as the victims of 'shell-shock'. By the time the Irish Division had sailed away from Gallipoli, it had experienced some 8,000 casualties, including 3,000 fatalities. Soon afterwards the whole Gallipoli enterprise was abandoned by the British generals and the bodies of so many of the campaign's victims were left to moulder in shallow graves under makeshift crosses until, in the post-war years, the British Forces' Graves Registration unit began the process of creating military cemeteries in this tragic but beautiful landscape.

Sadly, Thomas Deddis, who had survived the horrors of Gallipoli, did not manage to survive the campaign which followed it. The soldiers of the 10th Division were sent to Salonika in order to defend the city from Bulgarian attack, and would spend much of the next two years in a Macedonian and Serbian landscape, where they would fight on the snow-covered Balkan hills at Kosturino, and also in the malarial swamps of the Struma valley. The precise circumstances of the demise of Thomas Deddis are not at all clear. He is recorded as having died of wounds in a hospital in Salonika on 5 June 1917, and he lies buried in a Commonwealth Graves war cemetery in that Greek city, at the other end of Europe from the island where he had been born, and where he had enlisted in the innocent and patriotic days of the summer of 1914. Sadly, few today remember that Irishmen and Bulgarians once fought a war. Few from County Down make a visit to the cemeteries of Salonika and Gallipoli, where the bones of numerous young men from this part of Ireland still lie beneath a Mediterranean sky.

The Great War was perhaps the single most influential and disruptive event in modern history. Not only did it send young men like Thomas Deddis across Europe to die for the British Empire, it also led to the collapse of imperial and monarchical power all across the Continent. The British Empire first began to unravel in Ireland and by the 1920s a new Irish Free State had been created, which wished to create a new national narrative, freed from the weight of British militarism. The story of the 10th Division at Gallipoli would be an unwanted piece of history. Even in the north, the much more symbolic and well-recorded slaughter of the Ulster Division at the Somme would be the main focus of commemoration, rather than the deaths of men like Thomas Deddis in Macedonia and at Gallipoli.

It is one of the wonders of a building such as Down County Museum that so much of European history may be grasped through an understanding of all that has happened within its walls. Perhaps it is time to acknowledge the young men who walked from various parts of the county to Downpatrick in the summer and autumn of 1914 and, here on the Mall, found themselves at the beginning of a journey which would end beneath a military gravestone in a foreign land. Sadly, all across the world, young men from a variety of national backgrounds walked to their nearest military barracks and did the same. In that sense, the building which now houses our museum was once witness to the beginning of Europe's most primal 20th century tragedy.

Philip Orr teaches English and Drama at Down High School, Downpatrick. In May 2005 Philip will be launching a new book entitled *The Field of Bones: The Lost Story of an Irish Division at Gallipoli*, published by Lilliput Press

The Kilmainham Gaol 'Ballykinlar Collection'

Niamh O'Sullivan

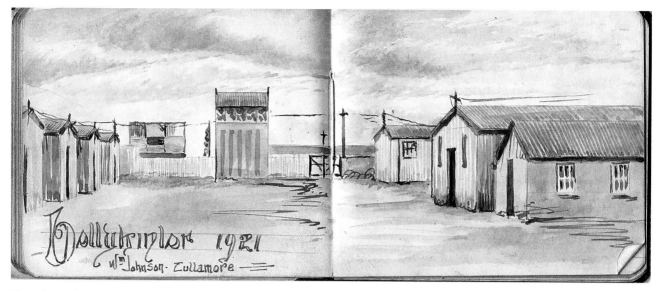

Sketches of Ballykinlar Camp and the prisoners'
chapel from Henry Dixon's autograph book
(Courtesy of Kilmainham Gaol Archives)

Hugh Deery from Letterkenny, Co Donegal,
was interned in Ballykinlar Camp, Co Down[1], for
twelve months during the Anglo-Irish War
(1919–1921). His presence there makes the episode
rather more personal for the staff in Kilmainham
Gaol Museum, as he is the great-grand uncle of one
of our guides, Sean Browne. Sean tells a familiar
story – Hugh Deery never spoke much of his time
in Ballykinlar, leaving his family then and now to
wonder what conditions must have been like for the
various men held in this '*barbed wire cage*', as
many inmates referred to Ballykinlar.

We are instead left hoping for any manner of
surviving evidence – solid material which has
lasted the course of time and which will speak for
itself of events that occurred in the camp. In the
Kilmainham Gaol Archives, we are fortunate
enough to possess a quantity of such evidence, in
the form of three internment orders sending
prisoners Ernest Noonan (19 LG 1C26 08), John
Hopper (19 LG 1K42 30) and Peter Byrne (19 LG
1K53 14) to Ballykinlar; two old school-type
exercise books containing a Roll of Men in Camp
Two Ballykinlar 1921 (19 MS 1B41 06) and a

School Roll (19 MS 1B41 05). There is an essay,
*Barbed Wire Photography (How it was done in
Ballykinlar)* (19 MS 1B41 10), with
accompanying smuggled photographs. There are
also a number of autograph books, owned and
circulated by the prisoners themselves, with their
usual contents of prisoners' names, cheery lines,
quotations (in a swift overview quotes by P H
Pearse, Thomas Davis and Eamon de Valera can

'More camp rumours' from Ballykinlar autograph book (Courtesy of Kilmainham Gaol Archives)

all be located), much needed humorous observations and drawings both in black and white and colour.

One particularly striking autograph book in the Kilmainham Gaol Ballykinlar Collection is that which was presented to Henry Dixon (19 MS 1C25 11) by his fellow prisoners in Ballykinlar. A Dublin solicitor, Henry Dixon had also been interned in Frongoch Camp in Wales after the 1916 Rising – he was the Frongoch Camp librarian and already then over 70 years old. Although many pages of his autograph book are blank, there are some lists of prisoners, detailing their names and addresses, among whom 'our' Hugh Deery from Ballyboe, Letterkenny, Co Donegal, can be found. There are names representing Down (James McGlennon, Loughinisland), Dublin, Tyrone, Clare, Cork and even Liverpool (James McClean, Victoria Square). This larger than average autograph book contains many fine colour illustrations, including several views of the Camp itself and one of the altar made by the prisoners in their chapel in No 1 Camp.

A good example of the type of verse written by the prisoners can be found in an autograph book belonging to James Warren (19 MS 1C25 03) from Ballineen, Co Cork, who describes himself as *'Prisoner of War No 350 Hut 26 ...Ballykinlar Co Down, 1920 & 1921'*. Warren's fellow inmate John Bonner from Summerhill, Donegal, who was held in Hut 19, writes in the book:

> Just a line dear Comrade
> Your memory to recall
> The time you spent in prison
> With the Boys from Donegal
> I want you to remember me
> To all the boys from Cork
> Who made the name of Erin ring
> From Paris to New York
> I want to be remembered
> To comrades one and all
> Who fought to free old Ireland
> From Cork to Donegal.

There is a charming drawing by Eamon Hayes from *'Belfast and Ballykinlar Internment Camp'* in an unidentified autograph book (19 MS 1C25 04) which depicts a group of exotic birds in full colour huddled together talking amongst themselves, with the caption reading: *'More Camp Rumours – I hear we're getting out of the Cage to-morrow'*. This relates to the constant hopes the men cherished of being released, and is an excellent example of the finely tuned sense of humour shared by the prisoners, which formed a vital element in their survival.

The autograph book which belonged to Patrick Hayes (19 MS 1C25 10) is filled in completely in Irish, which emphasises the importance the prisoners set on their native language – Irish classes were held in Ballykinlar Camp. The

Altar set up in prisoners' chapel in Ballykinlar (taken with Ballykinlar camera) (Courtesy of Kilmainham Gaol Archives)

Kilmainham Ballykinlar Collection includes a copy of a certificate awarded to James Coleman for his Irish studies (19 MS 1D45 24) in the Camp. And what sacrifices did Tomas Ó h-Onan make when he pasted four differently coloured Ballykinlar Internment Camp money tokens into his autograph book (19 MS 1C24 01) valued at 1/-, 6d, 3d and 1d respectively? Each of the tokens has Tomas' prisoner number attached – No 130.

The *Barbed Wire Photography* essay tells the story of the seriousness with which the prisoners themselves approached the question of remembrance:

The continual hunt for souvenirs by the internees suggested to our photographer that perhaps he could satisfy to some extent the big demand for mementoes of the days spent inside 'the cage'. The laws under which we were forced to live barely permitted us to receive the ordinary necessities of life and a camera was one of the many luxuries which were declared forbidden.

The author relates how a camera was eventually smuggled into Ballykinlar:

...a substantial home-made cake arrived in the Camp and with the assistance of our representatives in the censoring department it escaped the piercing knife and eye of the military

Money tokens used in Ballykinlar Internment Camp saved and displayed in an autograph book (Courtesy of Kilmainham Gaol Archives)

Violin class, Ballykinlar (taken with Ballykinlar camera) (Courtesy of Kilmainham Gaol Archives)

censor. It was a well-made cake and the fact that a small folding camera was one of the principal ingredients did not affect its flavour.

He continues to relate more of the technical details involved in photography:

> With or without the consent of the Medical Officer the chemicals required for developing were found or manufactured in the chemist's laboratory attached to the hospital. A dark-room was easily obtainable as most of the huts were without light from night-fall till morning and after some time we were able to perform any task or odd job in the dark.

Some of the photographs (19 PO 1A32 07) appearing herewith are those taken with the Ballykinlar camera – a violin class with Conductors Martin Walton and Frank Higgins from No 1 Camp; and the altar in the prisoners' chapel, No 1 Camp, Ballykinlar. The essay finishes:

> ...the photographs exhibited here are enlarged reproductions of these same negatives and comparing the size of the negative with the big enlargements will give you an idea of the excellence of the work executed by 'The Ballykinlar Photographer'.

The Kilmainham Ballykinlar Collection also contains several copies of their Camp newspapers *Na Bac Leis* – the September (19 NW 1E11 06), October (19 NW 1D22 15) and November (19 NW 1E11 06) 1921 editions, and a single copy of *The Barbed Wire* for August 1921 (19 NW 1D23 28). *Na Bac Leis* (don't bother with that) consists of various articles, gardening notes, GAA notes, verses, and editorials. The September issue even has a cartoon strip where a prisoner is being sent home in the first frame but by the end he realises wistfully it has only been a dream! There is also a small boxed piece entitled *'Overheard at the Dail: When one of our T.D.'s was addressing the DAIL in Irish, somebody asked: "What Irish is that?" The answer came immediately – "The best Irish of all, my boy, Ballykinlar Irish."'*

Illustrating the difficulties of Camp journalism J S Considine has a verse in the October 1921 issue entitled: *'I wouldn't if I were you':*

> If appointed you were a CAMP JOURNAL to run,
> With a single machine and so much to be done,
> Would you take it – aye, e'en at the point of a gun.
> I wouldn't if I were you!

All issues conclude with the professional announcement: *Na Bac Leis – Printed and Published in No 1 Cage, Ballykinlar. Letters to the Editor should be sent to Hut 14!*

The November issue contains several pieces on the death of Tadhg Barry *'shot dead in Ballykinlar Camp 15th November 1921'*. A verse, by one of

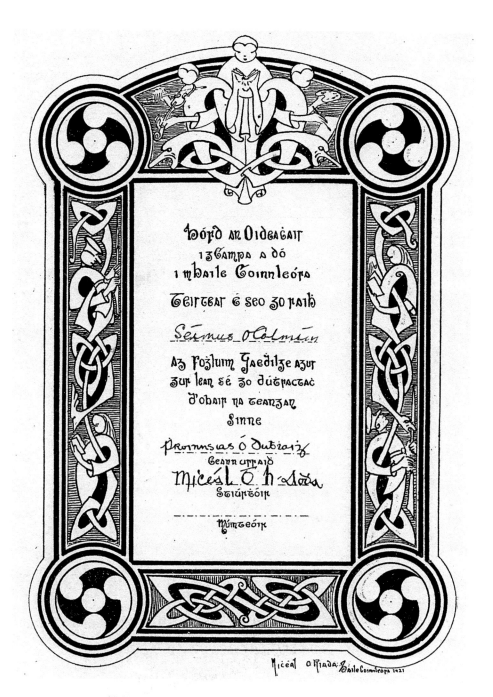

Irish certificate awarded to James Coleman, Ballykinlar Internment Camp (Courtesy of Kilmainham Gaol Archives)

the Camp's poets, J S Considine, begins:

> Hark to the Banshee's piercing caoine,
> O'er Ballykinlar's wind-swept shore,
> For Tadg – the peerless, noble Gael,
> Is now no more.

The GAA notes in this November issue mention the semi-final of the Hut Championship played by teams representing Huts 34 and 35, with the following description: *'During the game we were treated to some fine football...'*. Hut 34 were the winners! The article continues: *'The match between Huts 8 and 16 so much looked forward to, proved rather disappointing'*.

Unlike the typed *Na Bac Leis*, the only copy in the Kilmainham Ballykinlar Collection of *The Barbed Wire*, August 1921, is hand written. The front page consists of a number of quotations referring to future troubled times, among others:

> Don't worry. All's well. President De Valera's Cabinet is not made of Greenwood. Lloyd George proposes; Dail Eireann disposes ... and To discuss the subject before it is discussed by Dail Eireann is a stepping-stone to disgust.

The Editor of *The Barbed Wire* could be reached in Hut 21. This journal also has GAA notes and a small piece on the Camp Library, which was opened in January 1921 in No 2 Camp *'with a 'Capital' of about 100 books presented by internees'*. By this August issue, there were an estimated 2000 books on its shelves: *'The Barbed Wire was printed and published at the Ballykinlar Press for the proprietors. Irish paper and Irish labour only used – 19-8-21.'* They state tongue in cheek: *'Owing to pressure on our space we are obliged to hold over many articles, notes and advertisements.'*

Finally, the Kilmainham Ballykinlar Collection also contains letters written by Peter (O') Byrne to his wife Frances, who lived in Barrow Street, Dublin (19 LR 1B13 18, 19 LR 1B13 19 and 19 LR 1B13 17). Peter was in No 33 Hut in No 2 Camp and he wrote regularly every week to Frances, both business and personal letters, from December 1920 until December 1921. His letters range from a mixture of the very ordinary to the very astute, as he confides his hopes and his fears together with words of practical advice to his far-away wife.

In early December 1920 he writes that he was placed in Hut 37 No 1 Camp when he arrived on the Friday morning. He tells Frances: *'I have just heard when writing that we will have to supply our own notepaper and stamps'*. On 16 January 1921 he was moved to No 2 Camp. In February he informs Frances that all letters coming and going are censored *'before you or I get them'*. In March he explains how *'25 of us sleep in each Hut'*. On 7 April he writes: *'I have no strange news as everything and everyday is the same in this Hell of the Damned Place'*. By 25 April he has cheered up somewhat:

> ...there was an election here for a new Hut Leader which means one man in charge of each Hut of 25 men. I was elected by 16 votes to 9 so you see I am a favourite with the men.

One of the most difficult aspects of life in Ballykinlar was the awful uncertainty, the wondering when the men would eventually be released. Peter refers to this in a letter in May, in which he tells Frances he expects *'to be home in perhaps a fortnight, but certainly in a month'*. In most of his letters he now refers to his expectations of getting home soon. By 23 May he writes: *'... things here are not a bed of roses as we are not getting on well here at all... We got a lot of knocking about here on Saturday night last and*

some of our men were arrested and put in the guardroom. I have no idea when things will settle down but I hope soon'*. In June he describes Ballykinlar to Frances: *'This place is nothing to boast about as we can see nothing but barbed wire here and plenty of that. We never see anyone from outside.'*

He mentions things like attending Irish and dancing classes, and tells Frances about the *'hundreds of bags'* (macramé) being made in all colours by the internees. On 11 July he mixes high political hopes with more mundane day-to-day issues:

> I hope everything will go on well with Dev and that we will have peace with honour if not I do not care to leave here...I want my country to come out of this conference with that honour which she has never lost...And all in Ireland love and trust Eamon as we know him well by now...I get up about 8 and go to Mass. Then I have not to soil my hand for the whole day nothing to do only make the bags or lie in the sun.

He continues on 21 July: *'...you forget that I am inside a barbed wire cage here and never see the outside world and it is a hell of a place I would sooner be in jail than this place.'* A few days later, still with that ever present hope of early release he writes: *'I will wear my own grey trousers going home as I don't want any of their stuff on my back when I leave here.'* His hopes of getting out soon are still alive on 1 August: *'I expect things to go very quick now as we have seven DAIL members in this camp.'* He continues on a more despairing note: *'I have not had a decent feed since the 23rd of November last as we never get enough. But after going through last winter we can stand anything.'* Three days later he seems still gripped by this despair: *'...we have no comfort of any description. I hope things will be settled soon as this place is setting some poor men wrong in the head in fact the best of us are a little gone already...if we are here for next winter it will be the death of some of us this is the worst Hell ever was made.'*

Towards the end of August he is in a more political frame of mind as he writes to Frances: *'...the Country was never in better hands and our leaders are the best men on earth we trust them* and whatever they do we will all follow them as it would be better to die in the attempt to free our Dear Land than live a day longer as slaves', and, comparing himself with other figures from Irish history: '...but still if our poor Country wins her freedom what matter as a year or two is nothing when we think of poor Tom Clarke who done 20 years and Michael Davitt & O'Donovan Rossa and all they suffered we are suffering nothing compared to them'. But the months passed slowly by and on 3 October he briefly says: 'A fellow would be better in his grave than living in this hole', but he qualifies that somewhat by recognising on 17 October: 'I suppose you read in the papers about our treatment and that we are without bed boards we are lying on the floor for the past three weeks and so far as the blankets go we might as well have fishing nets over us as they are threadbare its our good humour that keeps us alive...'

Also in October he writes of the shooting of fellow internee Tadg Barry: 'I am very sorry to tell you that another of our poor comrades was shot here on Tuesday Tadg Barry', and '... if the enemy would only keep outside the cage and not be rushing in in the middle of the night and shouting that they will shoot us'. By the end of November he is again referring to the eventual release: 'but under no circumstances will I apply for parole as when I leave here I will leave as a free man.' At the beginning of December he simply states: '...we are in on the second year now.'

And so Peter Byrne, together with the autograph books and their humour and sketches, the camp journals and the surviving photographs, give us strong glimpses of life in Ballykinlar Camp, enabling us to find a way around the respectful silence of so many of the internees, including our own Hugh Deery. Peter reminds Frances, and through her, all of us, of the precarious existence he led in the Camp, in two letters from September 1921: 'I cannot tell you my troubles in this place enough to say I have plenty of it...I find it fits in better to try smiling as we have got tired praying for our enemy...' and 'I am sorry my letter of Thursday last went astray. You see we have to leave our letters open and the censor must have put the letters in the wrong envelopes'. The men would frequently impose their own limits on worried letters home, and the censor worked thoroughly. Nevertheless, we still succeed in penetrating somewhat the life in Ballykinlar Camp, at the start of the 1920s.

Niamh O'Sullivan graduated from University College Dublin and the King's Inns, and started work in the *Kilmainham Jail Restoration Society* in 1982. After the gaol was handed back to the State in 1986, she stayed on, and in 1992 commenced work as Kilmainham Gaol Archivist, where she has continued to work to the present.

Notes

1. As a result of the events of 21 November 1920, when Michael Collins' men assassinated fourteen British intelligence agents in Dublin, the British authorities set up Ballykinlar Internment Camp in County Down, applying strong new internment powers. From surviving Ballykinlar documents in the Kilmainham Gaol Archives, we can establish that Ballykinlar itself consisted of two camps– Camp Number One and Camp Number Two. *The Roll of Men in Camp Two* in the Kilmainham archives lists the 38 huts which made up that camp; other documents suggest Camp One had at least 37 huts. We know from a letter written by prisoner Peter (O') Byrne to his wife from Ballykinlar that each hut housed 25 men. These figures suggest that Ballykinlar Internment Camp had a capacity to hold up to at least 1875 prisoners. Peter (O') Byrne's final letter to his wife is dated December 1921– his stay in the camp therefore coincided roughly with its own life span– from late 1920 until December 1921, a short time after the signing of the Treaty on 6 December. In subsequent years, Ballykinlar was used by both the UDR and the Royal Irish Regiment.

The Life and Loss of the SS *Upas* of Newry

Sean Patterson

The SS *Upas* (Courtesy of Glasgow University Archive Services, DC101/1609)

Launched on 21 February 1913 and completed in April of that year, the SS *Upas* of Newry was designed as a modern small coaster for trading in the Irish Sea. She was the pride of the fleet of J S Fisher of Newry, and built by Fullerton's of Paisley to a much higher specification than the other small coasters owned by the company. At 168 foot long she was considerably longer than the standard Newry Collier of 142 foot (the maximum length that could be accommodated by the Ringsend Dock in Dublin where Fishers had a lucrative coal contract). Indeed she appears to have been a direct replacement for the SS *Seapoint* of similar dimensions, which the company sold in 1911.

Powered by a two cylinder compound expansion engine built by Ross and Duncan, like most vessels in the fleet she had a working speed of about 12 knots. As with practically all coastal traders of her era, all power on board the vessel was provided by steam. Unlike her more humble sisters in the Fisher Fleet, she had both a steam windlass

to raise the anchor and a steam capstan to heave in her stem, as well as an enclosed charthouse directly below her open bridge. This is in direct contrast to other Newry steamers like the *Pine* and the *Alder* whose bridge stood on four stanchions with an open area below.

Although she may have been a modern collier by early 20th century standards, conditions aboard the *Upas* were primitive. There was no electricity on board; lighting was provided by oil lamps in the crew's quarters, and acelytene lamps in the engine rooms. The vessel was steered from an open bridge situated amidships, the only navigational aids being a compass and charts. The sole protection from the elements was a canvas sheet or 'dodger' which could be raised to eye level in very rough weather.

The seamen and firemen slept together in the forward end of the vessel below water level in the forecastle or foc'sle. The sole means of heating was a coalburning stove known as a 'bogey', and the

The superstructure and machinery of the *Upas* was in stark contrast to the SS *Pine* also owned by Fishers and built in 1907 (Courtesy of Sean Patterson)

only lighting, paraffin lamps. Paddy McKeown from Newry worked on the SS *Rowan* of Newry, built in 1932 but identical in almost every respect to the *Upas*. He described conditions in the foc'sle:

> On a dirty night you couldn't light the bogie ... with the pounding of the ship. Every time she plunged you got the smoke ... you could smell the clothes ... I mind even as a child I could smell my father (who also worked for Fishers) coming in ... I could smell the paraffin oil.

Johnny Byrne worked on Fisher's vessels at about the same time as the *Upas* was in service. He told an interviewer for Radio Ulster:

> It was all oil then... paraffin oil, and the fumes from it and the fumes that were coming off the stove were anything but sweet!

The crew slept in wooden bunks on a straw mattress commonly known as a 'donkey's breakfast'. Dan Brennan, who joined the SS *Pine* of Newry in 1930, commented:

> After you had it a couple of weeks, it just looked like a pancake.

On the *Upas* the cooking was done in the galley on the rear or 'after' end of the ship. However, after working a shift or watch of four hours on an open

bridge on a cold night, many crewmen headed off to a large grate which sat above the ship's boiler, known as the 'fiddley'. Dan Brennan commented that it was a great spot for drying your clothes:

> I suppose if it wasn't for the fiddley, the lot of us would have died.

The Captain had his own cabin amidships on the starboard side of the ship while the First Mate had almost identical accommodation on the portside. Both cabins were directly below the chartroom and both men shared a common mess room. Further aft, the First Engineer had his own cabin on the portside adjacent to that of the Second Engineer. Both men's cabins were, for practical purposes, above the engines.

The ship's log for the *Upas* from July 1913 to 31 December 1913 gives some idea of the conditions of service of the crew, who agreed to work overtime 'where and when required by the master'. The Captain's weekly wage was £3.15.0 (the modern equivalent being £3.75 pounds sterling). The First Mate's wage was £2.00, the Second Mate's £1.14.6 (£1.72), an Able-bodied Seaman's was £1.12.6 (£1.62), and a Ship's Boy's wage was £1.00. The First or Chief Engineer was paid £2.15.0 (£2.75) the Second Engineer £2.00, and a

Bridge Street in Newry, where Captain McFerran, James McShane and William Leary lived. This row of houses is still referred to in Newry as Fisher's Row because of the number of seamen who lived in it in the employment of J S Fisher (Courtesy of Sean Patterson)

Fireman earned the same wage as an Able-bodied Seaman.

After her delivery, the *Upas* was employed on the coal trade, although she spent the summer months of 1913 on the south coast of England trading to France, probably carrying strawberries or potatoes, before returning to the coal run, which was the bedrock of Fisher's trade. An examination of her log between August and November 1913 shows that she was engaged exclusively in home waters, visiting ports such as Ayr, Irvine, Belfast, Sligo, Ardrossan, Waterford, Orme's Head, (where stone was loaded), Swansea, Harrington, Garston, Liverpool, Cardiff, Warrenpoint and her home port of Newry. When fully loaded, she drew fourteen feet of water, although her normal draught was 13'6", which was the maximum draught permitted for the Newry Ship Canal.

On St Patrick's Day 1915, at around 10pm, she left Ayr bound for Warrenpoint with a cargo of small coal, or 'nuts'. On board were eight crewmen, Captain William McFerran of Dundalk, her master, Samuel Hanna of Kilkeel, her First Mate, and James McShane of Newry, her Second Mate. Samuel Hollywood of Fathom acted as Able-bodied Seaman, and Joseph Hanna of Kilkeel (brother of Samuel) as Ordinary Seaman. The Chief Engineer was William Leary of Bridge Street, Newry, the Second Engineer was William Gallagher of Warrenpoint, and the Fireman was Edward Rocks of Newry. The *Upas* was one crew-member short. Apparently he had not joined her when leaving Newry, where she set off for the Point of Ayr in Wales, picked up a cargo of stone and set sail for Ayr, to collect coal for the return journey to Warrenpoint.

Samuel Hanna, in a radio interview[1], later told of how he had come on watch around midnight. Before he left the bridge at 4am, he altered course to allow the *Upas* to pass the South Rock Lightship on her starboard side and avoid going on the shore side of the lighthouse, which would run the risk of going aground. There was a heavy sea running at the time and shortly after the South Rock Lightship had been picked up, heavy snow drastically reduced visibility, so much so that, according to Samuel Hanna, the crew could see nothing at all. He commented that they *"could hardly see the foremast"*.

With the wind, and against the tide in a southeasterly gale, conditions were rough and, according to Hanna, the *Upas* was shifting a lot of water. Despite being built to quite a high specification, the *Upas*, it appears, was not a good sea boat. She was a tender or stiff boat, tending to roll heavily in strong seas. Because of this, and fearing he might run inside the lightship, Captain McFerran decided to 'heave to' or stop the vessel until visibility cleared, before proceeding on the remainder of the passage.

To do this entailed bringing the ship's bow into the wind, and consequently he asked Hanna to tell the Chief Engineer to raise more steam to enable the manouevre to be carried out. It was about six o'clock, just as day was breaking. Hanna told the BBC interviewer:

Captain McFerran was afraid of a scenario like this, when in 1924, the SS *Oak* of Newry was stranded on rocks in Cemae's Bay (Courtesy of Sean Patterson)

The tide was running against the wind, and made the sea very short and sharp, a short top on it.... It's just about the worst place it could be.

As Captain McFerran attempted to bring the *Upas* around, she *"got into the trough of the sea and she fell off one into the other and just fouled herself and turned over on her side and shifted the cargo"*[2]. Coal was a cargo, which like grain, was liable to move or shift in heavy weather making the vessel unstable. Perhaps the tender or stiff nature of the *Upas* herself may have contributed to this mishap. Just 13 years earlier another Newry vessel, the steamer *Cloughmore* had perished in Lough Swilly, along with six of her crew as a result of her cargo of grain shifting in bad weather.

The vessel almost capsized as she rolled and her cargo moved almost completely to her port side, leaving the steamer with a very dangerous list. Because of the severity of the list, the vessel could not steer. Captain McFerran left the bridge and met Hanna, reportedly saying: *"Its all up, she's quit steering."*

With no steerage, a heavy list to port, and with a south-easterly gale blowing, the ship and her crew were in grave danger. The steamer was filling up with water, so much so, that Hanna was unable to retrieve lifebelts from either his own cabin or the foc'sle, where he reckoned there was already four to five feet of water. The two engineers were able to take their lifebelts from their cabins, which were at deck level. James McShane climbed into the after rigging, retrieved the two belts which hung there, took one for himself and gave the other to Edward Rocks, the 24 year-old Fireman. However,

a wave broke over the ship and washed Rock's belt overboard.

During this time, Hanna was adamant that there was no panic on board. Although distress flares were available, they were not used. The ship's ensign was inverted as a distress sign and her horn was sounded, though as the ship filled up, and the steam pressure dropped, this became fainter. It did awake many of the residents of Portavogie and Ballyhalbert, who as daylight dawned watched the stricken steamer drift along at the mercy of wind and tide. The vessel was close enough to shore for them to see the crew huddled around the boat deck.

It was decided to launch the port lifeboat. It was impossible to launch the two starboard lifeboats because of her severe list to port. The port boat, which Hanna said was "low in the water", was launched and several of the crew climbed into it. Because of the proximity of the lifeboat to the *Upas* and the fact that the ship was rolling heavily, Hanna used a boat hook to keep the lifeboat clear of the rolling coaster, in case the *Upas*' lifeboat davits caught it and capsized it.

The Chief Engineer, William Leary, attempted to jump into the boat but managed only to catch the side of it and called to Hanna for help. He in turn released the boat hook to grab Leary, the *Upas* rolled, her davits caught the boat and capsized it. The occupants were all thrown into the freezing sea. Hanna pushed himself clear of the steamer and swam towards a lifebelt which was floating in the sea. He believed it might have been the one McShane had given to Edward Rocks. McShane, a non-swimmer, was also in the water. He was being kept afloat with the aid of a lifebelt. Hanna, a strong swimmer, could see McShane, who was experiencing difficulties. Hanna told the radio interviewer:

He had to take what was coming and sometimes when the sea would have broke, he would have went away, maybe twenty feet.

However, in spite of the rough seas, it appears that the two of them remained together. Seemingly some of the crew remained on board the stricken steamer and some of those who were thrown into the water may have scrambled back aboard her. According to Hanna:

> The Captain... was on top of the boathouse... and I called onto him ... whether he answered or not, I didn't know. He just nodded the head. He wouldn't come down nor didn't come down. That's the last place I seen him, standing up there beside the boat on the starboard side.

Having been blown northwards, as far as Birr Point, the *Upas* was now blown backwards. Sinking deeper and deeper into the water, several of her crew huddled on her boat deck as she lay almost on her beam ends. Many of the onlookers on shore were fishermen, but their boats were on shore and it was impossible to put them to sea in such weather. Sara McVea, wife of the village postman, in the radio interview said:

> We were all on the knous, high up ... watching, and we could do nothing ... the people near Ballyhalbert saw the men on her, but they could do nothing for them at all. No small boat could have lived in the sea at that time.

Around 10:30am the Belfast Steamer, *Ailsa Craig*, en route from Belfast to Portarlington, spotted the *Upas*. Thomas Wilson, her captain, in an interview carried in the *Frontier Sentinel*[3], told how he saw the *Upas* off Burial Island, *"with a heavy list and gradually settling over"*. Due to the proximity of the *Upas* to the rocks, he could not bring his vessel directly to her aid and instead a lifeboat was launched with three crew members on board. He knew that the plight of the *Upas* was absolutely hopeless as *"the port rail was in the water altogether"*. He reported that two men were seen clinging to an upturned lifeboat but were washed off.

> The remaining men could be seen on deck and nothing could be done to help them.

Hanna and McShane had been, by Hanna's reckoning, in the water for about two and a half hours when the *Ailsa Craig*'s lifeboat reached them. He thought McShane *"was nearly finished"*. William Marks from Annalong, whom Hanna knew personally, reached out and pulled them into the boat saying: *"Sammy, you're all right yet!"*; and then helped McShane on board. When they were in the boat, Marks said to

Hanna: *"Look up Sammy, there's the last of her"*. In Samuel Hanna's own words:

> She seemed to slide back into the sea and then there was an explosion of some sort. I think it was the air in the hold with the pressure blew the hatches off ... there was nothing else, for there wasn't as much steam as would have blew it.

Captain Wilson on the *Ailsa Craig* reckoned that the remainder of the crew on the *Upas*, *"must have gone underneath with the suction created by the sinking ship."*

However for Hanna, McShane and the seamen from the *Ailsa Craig*, Marks, Adair and Torrens, the ordeal was not yet over. William Marks, in an interview with the *Belfast Telegraph*, on 15 December 1965 said:

> We were blown out to sea after we picked the men up, and had to bale the water out continuously.

By this time, the Donaghadee lifeboat had arrived on the scene, but the *Upas* was gone. The lifeboat picked up the five occupants from the *Ailsa Craig*'s boat, which was unable to return to the mother ship. The Donaghadee lifeboat was a welcome sight. Marks was of the opinion:

> We were picked up just in time, for we were nearly dead from the bitter cold.

They were to endure further hardship. The lifeboat was an open boat and because of the weather conditions, did not reach Donaghadee until 3.30 that afternoon. Before they left the scene, the crew of the lifeboat recovered a body, which they tried unsuccessfully to revive. This man, Hanna later found out, was William Gallagher, the Second Engineer. His fellow engineer, William Leary, was found washed ashore the following day.

After being tended to by nurses in the hotel in Donaghadee, Hanna took a walk in the town that evening before being brought to Warrenpoint by a relative of William Gallagher, whose coffined body accompanied them. The following morning he returned to Kilkeel without his younger brother, Joseph, whose body was never

The telegraph of the *Upas* salvaged from the wreck

recovered. William Gallagher is buried in Burren Cemetery, near Warrenpoint.

The *Upas* was the ninth Newry Collier to be lost between 1900 and 1915, and the fourth to suffer heavy loss of life. Surprisingly, it did not receive excessive coverage in the local papers. The column reporting the disaster in the *Frontier Sentinel*[4] was squeezed between news items on the 'Newry Christian Brothers' and 'Old St. Patrick's Days'. However, the following year another Newry steamer, almost identical to the *Upas*, was to make national headlines when she collided with a passenger steamer, the *Connemara* at the entrance to Carlingford Lough. She was the SS *Retriever*[5]. That collision on 3 November 1916 was to claim over ninety lives.

Sean Patterson is a primary school teacher and canal enthusiast and has a special interest in Newry maritime history.

Notes and References
1. 'There the Last of Her', BBC Radio Ulster, September 1978, also contains interviews with Sara McVea and John Byrne.
2. Ibid.
3. *The Frontier Sentinel*, a Newry Newspaper, 20 March 1916.
4. Ibid.
5. See my article in the *Down Survey*, 2002.

Acknowledgements
Without the help of the following this article would not have been possible: my father, the late Sean Patterson, who remembered the loss and first told me about it; my daughter, Catherine Patterson for typing the article; Ian Wilson, whose account of the disaster was the first I read on the matter, and who has been an invaluable help to me on all matters maritime; Paddy McKeown and Dan Brennan, both sadly passed away, who worked on Fisher's steamers; and John Fisher whose background information on the family fleet has also been invaluable.

The Kilkeel U-boat Incident of 1918

Bill Quinn

The *Mary Joseph* pictured in Kilkeel Harbour with Jim Pat Curran and John Mackintosh in the 1950s. She was later acquired by the Ulster Folk and Transport Museum (Courtesy of the Ulster Folk and Transport Museum)

On 17 May 1918 the Kilkeel fleet left the harbour to drift net for herring. As one of the boats was sailing to the fishing ground, a member of the crew noticed the compass was spinning. He drew the rest of the crew's attention to this, but nobody knew the cause of this strange phenomenon. The boats continued to the fishing ground. At daylight the next morning, on 18 May, a German submarine surfaced in the middle of the fleet, ordered the crews into the punts and told them to come along the side of the submarine.

They were then ordered on to the deck. One of the German officers then proceeded to place a bomb on each boat. The subsequent explosions sank the five boats. The names of the boats were *Never Can Tell*, *Jane Gordon*, *Cypress*, *St Mary*, and *Lloyd*. Some of the boats had no punt and the captain ordered them on to another fishing boat, the *Moss Rose*, and let them row for home. The mystery of the spinning compass was revealed. The owners received no compensation for the loss of their boats, although their local MP fought hard for them.

The *Mary Joseph* was not fishing in the same area, and so she wasn't seen by the submarine, but the folk at home thought she had been sunk also, as she did not return to harbour until the end of the week, to great rejoicing.

Many years later, in 1952, a reporter came to write an article on the lost boats. She went to Tommy Donnan as she heard he was a crew member of the *Never Can Tell*. The conversation went something like this:

"Are you Mr Tommy Donnan?" Tommy answered: "Yes". "Are you the Tommy Donnan who was a crew member of the *Never Can Tell* when she was sunk?" Tommy answered: "No". The reporter said: "I was led to believe you were the last surviving member of the *Never Can Tell*." To which Tommy replied: "I was not aboard the *Never Can Tell* when she sank – but I was aboard about 15 minutes before she sank!"

Bill Quinn is a former Kilkeel boatbuilder and takes a keen interest in all things relating to the history of Kilkeel.

Portaferry Portraits: A Photographic Collection, 1900–1930

Colm Rooney

Portrait of Eliza-Ann McAfee, 1920s
(Courtesy of Colm Rooney)

The article 'Down through the Lens' by Lesley Simpson and Allen Thompson which appeared in the 2001 issue of *Down Survey* gave an account of the invention and development of photography. It also outlined the Museum's photographic archive and some of its gaps: 'More images from the early 20th century would be welcomed' and 'we would like to see the ... eastern part of the county better represented'.[1]

It was in this context that I thought of the collection of photographs left by my grandmother, Eliza-Ann McAfee (née McMullan). She was born in Portaferry in 1905, moved to Strangford in about 1930 (one of the shorter migrations in recorded history) and died there in 1992. The one hundred or so photographs cover family, friends and everyday life from the late 19th century until her move to Strangford. Two photographs from

the collection, showing marine salvage workers of the firm of McCausland, were reproduced in *Down Survey* 2002.

In 1839 photography was a mysterious and pioneering new technology. It developed rapidly over the succeeding decades and by the end of the 19th century photographers' studios were a common sight on high streets all over the country. Even hand-held personal cameras were becoming available at a reasonable cost by the early years of the 20th century.[2]

If the photographs in this collection are in any way representative, they show that the studio-portrait was still predominant in Portaferry even into the 1920s. Wartime portraits were taken to send back to families showing their sons and brothers looking proud and suitably martial in

Two soldiers, one Willie Hill of Portaferry, during the First World War (Courtesy of Colm Rooney)

Maggie, a munitions worker in Kilmarnock, 1916–7 (Courtesy of Colm Rooney)

The McMullan boys, c1900, prior to the emigration of the family to the United States (Courtesy of Colm Rooney)

their uniforms. A notable feature of social change during the First World War was the large-scale emancipation of women from domestic work and their employment in a wide range of factory jobs, particularly the munitions industry. I well remember my grandmother, whose elder sister Nellie worked in a munitions plant in Scotland, describing the dangers of this work– the necessity for wearing one's hair closely bound so as to prevent 'scalping' by the fast-turning lathes. One of the photographs shows 'Maggie', a friend of Nellie's, in her work clothes.

Portaferry had very strong links with Scotland, with many family members making the journey in search of work. Many photographs in the collection are by Glaswegian photographers. Some particularly poignant portraits show families just prior to their emigration to the New World.

The information on the back of those

Lily Bones, friend of Eliza-Ann, 1915–7 (Courtesy of Colm Rooney)

Cassie Daly, friend of Eliza-Ann, August 1915
(Courtesy of Colm Rooney)

Lizzy McKeag, friend of Eliza-Ann, August 1915
(Courtesy of Colm Rooney)

photographs taken by Belfast or other local studios is exceptionally helpful as W A Maguire's book, *A Century in Focus*, allows these to be dated more accurately. These photographs give us a glimpse of the clothing and hair-styles of the period and of how these Portaferry people looked on their trips to Belfast and Bangor during, and in the decade or so before and after, the First World War. They were probably the first generation of their families to have their photographs taken and it is pleasing that they have survived to bear witness to an era that is rapidly passing out of living memory.

Colm Rooney is a schoolteacher and a regular contributor to the publications of the Lecale Historical Society.

Notes
1. *Down Survey*, 2001 pp 62-71.
2. W.A. Maguire, *A Century in Focus: Photography and Photographers in the North of Ireland 1839–1939*, Belfast, 2000. This work is highly recommended to those who wish to know more about the subject and has been invaluable in helping to date some of the photographs in this article.

Local Stories from the First World War

Samuel Hoy (1893–1916) joined the 11th Battalion Royal Irish Rifles and was based at Clandeboye Camp, before leaving for France. It was while he was at Clandeboye that he wrote the letter illustrated. He was killed at the battle of the Somme, aged 23. We would like to thank Mrs Eileen Lewis, Samuel Hoy's niece, for this information and for letting us copy the photograph and letter.

Clandeboye Camp
16/2/16

Dear Father Just a few lines hoping to find you well well as it leaves me the same we are still heave as yet So I will likely be up on Sat. Walter has been put into the Draft again so he will likely be going along with us. I had a letter from Ballyclover this week & the are all well there. I Suppose the cattle is not getting & cheaper

I hope my mother & Bessie is keeping well & all the rest of you hoping to see you all on Sat your Son No 9 Rfm S Hoy no 6 Hut B Coy 18ᵗʰ Batt R I R Clandeboye Camp

John Edmund Warnock (1887–1971) entered the Royal Garrison Artillery in 1914 at the outbreak of war and served for over three years in France. He reached the rank of Major and Commanding Officer of 498 Siege Battery BEF. During his time in France he was shot down from a balloon and buried by a shell explosion, sustaining severe injuries which persisted for several years.

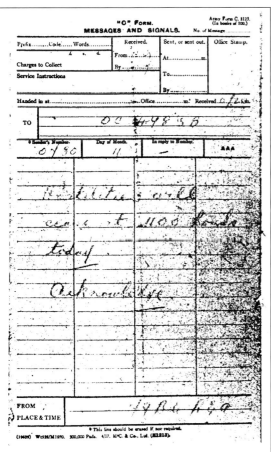

498 SIEGE BATTERY, B.E.F.

A Christmas card sent from 498 Siege Battery, and a telegram informing the Commanding Officer of 498 Siege Battery that the war was over: 'Hostilities will cease at 1100 hours today. Acknowledge.' We would like to thank Mrs Joy Maxwell, Major Warnock's daughter, for this information and for letting us copy the photograph, card and telegram.

The Summer of 1917: How the Bangor Paper saw it

Ian Wilson

Bangor Family loses three sons. Our reader will join us in extending sincerest sympathy to Mr and Mrs Angus, 20 Albert Street, who have just received notification of the death of their third son, Rifleman Blair Angus. Until now they had always hoped that since he was posted missing he would turn up to them. This makes a clean sweep of all the boys in the family. James Angus, of the Canadians, was killed on 15 September 1916 and Robert on 19 July 1916, and now the death of the youngest boy Blair on 1 July is officially notified (Co Down Spectator, June 15, 1917).

North Down Heritage Centre holds two valuable sources for the First World War, all the back numbers for the *Co Down Spectator* since 1913, and a very fine Memorial Book picturing all men of the town and district who died in the conflict. This was donated in 1998 by the local branch of the Royal British Legion. Using the local paper to follow up the brief facts below each serviceman's photograph results in finds like the above: a brief item in the weekly 'District News' column. 'A clean a sweep of all the boys'. Could there be a more chilling choice of words, laden with overtones of war as the grimmest of reapers? Blair Angus was one of the 24 Bangor soldiers killed on the first day of the Somme offensive. However, rather than looking again at this, the worst of bad times, my intention is to examine how the *Co Down Spectator* in the summer of 1917 was reporting the war, and life, which, as is its way, did go on:

Bangor people are indignant at the Rev. R. M Kerr for bringing his brass band and disturbing the Pierrots. A man (and a Christian) like Mr Kerr ought to have some consideration for other people's rights.

Two other weekly features are 'My Column' and 'Town Tattle', seemingly, by their pompous and right-wing style, from the same pen. In 'My Column' the author has license to roam beyond parochial matters and comment on national and international affairs. Socialists outrage him. Ramsay McDonald and colleagues are being hindered trying to reach an international Socialist conference in neutral Sweden :

The sailors' embargo on Ramsay McDonald has succeeded. He and Mr Jovett are back in Westminster, passports and all. Probably they will now try to reach Sweden by aeroplane. Had they just thought of it in time they may have got over with the German machines which slaughtered the English babies on Wednesday. By the way, Mrs Pankhurst has apparently got away all right. Than either of the male delegates, I have more faith in her voicing the true sentiments of the British people.

Unlike the *Spectator* in the Second World War, the papers in 1914–18 contain much about the course of the action. Almost nothing is reported in the later conflict. Even obituaries tend only to state 'on active service', whereas in some cases, as we will see, detailed accounts of circumstances are printed in 1914–18. The first air raids on London and the south-east were occurring in 1917, as mentioned in the above extract, a very modern threat, and an awesome spectacle (depicted in a famous painting by Sir John Lavery). The *Spectator* prints a Press Association account:

Magnificent but terrifying sight... The sky as if by magic became darkened by the sable wings of the ministers of death...

Summer 1917 papers have column after column of small print reporting the action: *'The Messines Triumph'; 'Second Army's Gallantry'; 'Sir Douglas Haig's Tribute: Long step Nearer the Final Victory'*. Yet it is easy to detect that, since the heady days of August 1914, people had become accustomed to the war, and resigned to its toll:

We have often regretted the lukewarm manner in which drafts from Clandeboye camp are sent off at Bangor station. The crowd that sees them off are sympathetic, no doubt, but their cold sadness is depressing. We would rather hear a cheer with warm wishes for a safe return... There is one silver lining in the dark cloud and that is the organisation for which Mrs Roy of Belfast Road, Bangor, is responsible, whereby each man who leaves for the front is presented with a gift of cigarettes.

Reading these fascinating papers may suddenly throw up questions one has never thought of. In all the enduring commemoration of the number of Ulstermen who fought in the war, aren't historians forgetting the young men who didn't join up? What percentage did they form? The easy image is of masses enlisting in the 36th Ulster Division and departing for France. You just never hear about people who weren't involved in major events. But some earned a stern rebuke in 'Town Tattle':

> I must remark on the number of deserving Scottish visitors who have faced the dangers of U-boats to cross for a quiet holiday in Bangor. I was pained on the other hand to see so many evident young slackers parading the streets of the town in a hopelessly intoxicated condition. What our quiet Scottish friends will have to say I do not know.
> Parents who have given their sons to the Empire might justly be pardoned for condemning the blatant and callous conduct of these slackers who indulge in noisy rowdyism but ought to be doing their bit in France...

And not everyone who joined up got to France. In the Memorial Book, the place Corporal Bertie Lytle died, Orange, California, provides a puzzle which the *Spectator* solves. A member of the Cycling Corps (perhaps from his 'quiet and unassuming' nature, not the most promising fighting man) he fell ill while training at

Corporal Bertie Lytle, from the Bangor (Co Down) War Memorial Album 1914–1919 (Courtesy of North Down Heritage Centre)

Clandeboye, was invalided out, and had been sent to California in November 1915 in an attempt to regain his health.

This case raises pertinent questions about the criteria for inclusion in the Memorial Book– and, indeed, the often vexed question about eligibility for town War Memorials. Currently, the criteria for the proposed register of all Irish First World War casualties need to be clearly established. Is it the place where a person was born, or their home at the time of their demise, which qualifies them for inclusion? What about those who died of after-effects, perhaps years later? And what of poor Bertie Lytle, who had been invalided out without seeing action? A case in point is Private Richard O'Brien, RIR, whose brief obituary appears on 16 July 1917. He does not appear in the Memorial Book, although he is described as formerly in the employment of Sir Samuel Davidson, as a gardener at his 'Seacourt' villa overlooking Bangor Bay.

What else was perturbing the *Spectator* that summer?

'My Column', staunchly Unionist (of course) grumbled:

> The USA in the declaration of their war aims addressed to Russia stipulate that no people must be forced to live under a sovereignty under which it does not wish to live. Clearly if the US authorities are consistent they cannot approve of Ulster being forced under a Dublin Parliament. Talking of America reminds me a certain Mr Hudson claims to have invented a device whereby U-boat torpedoes may be rendered harmless...

Gigantic world events share the columns with the politics of the parish pump. The Scottish visitors, having risked attack by U-boats, could not on arrival play cricket in Ballyholme Park as the Council had rejected an application to organise it *'on the grounds of danger to persons in the park or on the roadway'.*

Police swoop on owners of unlicensed dogs: *'defendant stated he thought the dog was going to die'; 'defendant stated that as he bought the dog from Mr Page who lived beside the police station he felt sure it would have been licensed'.* On one occasion the exigencies of war intrude, even into the sleepy proceedings of Bangor Petty Sessions :

> A Russian Jewess named Cecilia Leventon was summonsed for failing to report her arrival to the police. Defendant's daughter, who appeared a very intelligent girl, said her mother did not understand English thoroughly. Constable Sheridan said he thought defendant's intentions had been good. He would not like to be too hard on these quiet Jewish folk. The kind remark of the Constable melted the young woman to tears.

(She was fined two shillings and sixpence, with one shilling costs).

It would be interesting to know the story of these people – and also how, in pre-technological times, Constable Morrison 'proved' that motorist Hector Mitchell, 20 Atlantic Avenue, Belfast, was exceeding the 6 mph speed limit on seafront roads!

So the summer of 1917 passes: *'The Twelfth Anniversary'; 'Eloquent sermon by Rev. J.A. Carey'; 'Monster Demonstration at Hogstown'; 'Some Trenchant Speeches'; 'London Again Bombed'; 'Golf Club Red Cross Fete'; 'Alleged Larceny of a Bicycle'; 'Pacifist Meeting Broken Up. Wild scenes at Church'; 'Labour and Prohibition'* (the unions were firmly for it!).

But almost every issue carries news of fatalities among local men, almost all soldiers, although quite a bit appears about the torpedoing of the SS *Belgian Prince*, of which Bangor man Captain Henry Hassan is master. The soldiers are by no means all young 36th Ulster Division men. Sergeant Henderson, an 'old soldier' as the paper describes him, had 34 years' service when he lost his life. He is stated to have been an employee of the 'Picture Palace', Bangor's first cinema. More detail appears in the obituary of Rifleman John G Savage, RIR, younger son of Councillor James H Savage, a local building contractor. Some miles north-east of Ypres, the dugout in which he was a medical attendant received a direct hit. A few weeks later, the *Spectator* prints a letter from another local man, Sergeant J A Neill, who witnessed the explosion– in fact, it was towards the sanctuary of the dug-out he was crawling in a wounded state. The whole tone of the reporting is violently anti-German, and much is made of the allegedly deliberate shelling of a Red Cross post. Awful, rabidly anti-German verses are printed from time to time, perhaps locally-penned, perhaps syndicated.

News comes through of the death, while a POW at Caudry, of Rifleman Leslie Newell, RIR, from wounds received on the first day of the Somme offensive over a year before. His brother Hugh had been killed in the Dardanelles campaign of 1915. In 'District News' the entry is awarded the same space as 'A Giant Butterfly at Gray's Hill'– but what, really, more could be reported? Certainly the paper's style is austere and formal compared to today, but the human side, the crushing blows families received, do come through:

Captain Henry Hassan, from the Bangor (Co Down) War Memorial Album 1914–1919 (Courtesy of North Down Heritage Centre)

Sergeant William Henderson, from the Bangor (Co Down) War Memorial Album 1914–1919 (Courtesy of North Down Heritage Centre)

Rifleman James Savage, from the Bangor (Co Down) War Memorial Album 1914–1919 (Courtesy of North Down Heritage Centre)

Rifleman Leslie Newell, from the Bangor (Co Down) War Memorial Album 1914–1919 (Courtesy of North Down Heritage Centre)

Lt Knox Barrett, from the Bangor (Co Down) War Memorial Album 1914– 1919 (Courtesy of North Down Heritage Centre)

On Tuesday afternoon official information was received by Mr James H Barrett, Petty Session Clerk, Bangor, that his eldest son, Lieutenant Knox Barrett, Royal Field Artillery, had been killed in action on 20 September. Deceased was the eldest son of three soldier sons, two of whom have now made the supreme sacrifice, his younger brother Captain E W Barrett, of the Royal Flying Corps, having been killed in action on 29 May 1916. The youngest and only surviving son, Second Lieutenant St Clair Barrett, is now serving with the Royal Irish Fusiliers in France (27 September 1917).

'Town Tattle' adds more details about Lieutenant Knox Barrett:

...at the outbreak of the war he was in the service of the Hong Kong and Shanghai Bank, and immediately returned to the old country to do his bit. I met him on the morning of his leaving Bangor on receipt of instructions from the War Office. A finer lad I have seldom met...

Bangor Urban District Council also discussed the family's plight:

The Chairman Mr John McMeekan said that with regard to Mr Barrett's sacrifice he thought some action should be taken if possible to get that last son brought home (hear, hear) and, if not relieved of Army duties he might be put on some form of home service. If it would be possible for the Council to bring influence to bear to get that accomplished, it would be a kindness to Mr.

Barrett. One's blood boils, continued Mr McMeekan, when one thinks of what some families did while others did nothing...Mr Barrett is living in constant dread of another telegram...

Almost all families have heard handed-down tales of the First World War. My mother can just remember Uncle Samuel, somehow made ill by the war and dying young; also, a boy at her school they called 'Kitchy', named after Lord Kitchener; and the stories her mother told her of the horror of the approach of a bicycle boy with a telegram...

St Clair Barrett survived the war.

Ian Wilson is Manager of North Down Heritage Centre

Notes

1. The Bangor (Co Down) War Memorial Album 1914– 1919 is now on public display in North Down Heritage Centre, having been donated by the Bangor Branch, Royal British Legion (1998.005). The superbly crafted box originally containing it, bears a brass plaque stating the above title, and the name Bangor, Comrades of the Great War (the predecessor of the Royal British Legion). Listed are 124 local men, all with photographs, two per page. The book is approximately 400 mm x 200 mm (16 inches x 12 inches) and the pages are heavy card, interleaved with tissue paper. Prior to going on public display in 2000, much skilled specialist restoration work was undertaken by Cameron Preservation (Elgin Cameron), Lurgan.

Down in the War: County Down during the Second World War

M Lesley Simpson and Noel Hogg

To commemorate the 50th anniversary of the ending of the Second World War in 1945, Down County Museum opened an exhibition in 1995 called 'Down in the War'. In this we explored what life was like for people in County Down during the six years of war. Included were the stories of both residents and of those who came here from elsewhere, as refugees, or as part of the armed forces. The objects around which this exhibition was based have been added to since then and are included in the catalogue here.

Many County Down people left home to join the armed forces, while people from other parts of the world were stationed here. Camps and barracks were set up throughout the county. Although Belfast and Derry were the main wartime ports, fishing vessels were commandeered from County Down ports by the Royal Navy for carrying stores and taking people from the larger ships to shore. The crucial role played by the Royal Air Force in the Second World War explains the presence of Polish and Czech pilots at their bases in the county. Echoes of the personal and national tragedies of this time can be seen in quiet corners of County Down, such as the graveyards at Movilla and Ballycranbeg, where Polish airmen are buried. The buildings of the Old County Gaol in which our museum is now based, were used as barracks by the Welsh Fusiliers. America entered the war in December 1941 and their troops arrived in County Down in 1942. Some of them too were based here.[1]

With many young men away, women and older men were formed into support services, such as the Home Guard, Civil Defence and nursing organisations. Children made their own contribution; many helped out in the home or on the land, while in the cities they often left school early to work in factories. 'Make do and Mend' became a way of life. Factories concentrated on producing goods for the war effort and few items could be imported. With shortages and rationing, people found ingenious ways of 'making do' by recycling as much as possible.

Our exhibition commemorated all those who lived through the Second World War, as well as those who died. The dead included volunteers and conscripts in the armed forces of many countries, and civilians who were caught up in the war, including those millions murdered because of their race or culture. Each generation reviews and rewrites history. Facts must be sorted from opinion and propaganda, cause and effect analysed and memories compared. Some personal stories of local people were recorded at the time of this exhibition and a few are included below. Please help us to provide a balanced view by telling us your story, for the future, not just for this period of history but for others too.

Personal stories of the war

'I was stationed at Ballyhalbert with 504 Squadron for about six months in 1941. We provided air defence for Northern Ireland, taking part in convoy patrols, keeping watch for enemy aircraft taking photographs and for intruders generally'. *(Former Spitfire pilot, Cecil Austin).*

'My late husband, Alfie, was born in Holywood, County Down, in 1913. We met at Trinity College, Dublin, but Alfie went to Germany to continue his research. He had to leave in 1938, after enquiries from the Gestapo who were suspicious about his seemingly Jewish first name (Samuel). He trained as a weather forecaster for the RAF and we were married in Dublin in September 1941. Alfie was then posted to Wales and I travelled with him. Other postings included Uxbridge, Biggin Hill, West Malling and Dunstable. We returned to Northern Ireland to Ballyhalbert, County Down, then Derry and finally Belfast, where he was demobbed at the end of the war'. *(Mrs Dolly Scott, Belfast).*

'I joined the Royal Navy in 1940 but served on merchant ships in DEMS (Defensively Equipped Merchant Shipping). I served in several ships, from John Kelly ships to troop ships, from Ireland to East Africa, Burma and India'. *(Mr Harry Burnett, Ballygally, Downpatrick).*

Lieutenant Alfie Scott, weather forecaster in the RAF.

'After joining the WRNS (Wrens) and given some initial training, I was sent to Station X at Bletchley. We were working on code breaking but did not know until later that we were working with the famous 'Enigma' machines. It was exhausting work, standing all day, running immensely complicated machines. After several months, I was invalided out of the WRNS and later took on a secretarial post with the Durham Light Infantry Prisoners of War Fund. Our job was to keep prisoners in touch with their families and send parcels through the Red Cross'.[2] *(Miss Lydia de Burgh, Clough).*

'I was a nurse at No 2 Cargagh Camp during the war. People from Gibraltar were evacuated to Northern Ireland during the V-Bombing campaign on London in 1944. There were other camps at Saintfield, Crossgar and Clough in County Down, as well as in Counties Antrim and Londonderry. I particularly remember a 'Grand Amateur Vocal Concert' staged by members of these camps. The musical accompaniments were provided by a Gibraltarian String Orchestra'. *(Mary E Croskery, Downpatrick[3]).*

Combined Royal Navy and Royal Artillery Gun Crew on the *Dilwara*. Harry Burnett, from Strangford, is on the front row, fourth from the left.

Catalogue

Uniform and accessories

Uniform, Royal Air Force, comprising jacket, flying jacket, trousers, helmet and goggles, cap and ammunition pouch. These belonged to Neville Welch of Downpatrick, who was a Flight Lieutenant. He joined the RAF in 1939 and was demobbed in 1945. DCM 1998-69/1-6
Given by Mrs M Welch, Downpatrick.

Jacket, cap and epaulettes (from greatcoat), Royal Air Force, worn by the late Alfie Scott.
DCM 1987-146/1-3
Given by Mrs Dolly Scott, Belfast.

Uniform, Royal Navy, comprising:
Special mess dress jacket with tails and trousers. This was worn for full dress uniform. Ordinary mess dress jacket, waistcoat and trousers. This jacket was for daily wear. Cap and shoes. The cap was worn with anything except the full dress uniform and the shoes were worn with any outfit. These belonged to the donor who was a pilot in the Fleet Air Arm.[4]

Mess jacket of Gunner, belonged to Colonel J D Ferguson of Banbridge, 1939 period.
14 buttons, white metal, for Gunner's uniform. 1.9 cms diam.
DCM 1998-85/1-2, 1998-86/1-3, 1998-87 to 90, 1998-192
Given by Captain Michael Torrens-Spence, Downpatrick.

Battle jacket, army captain's. This may have belonged to a member of the Charley family of County Down.
DCM 1996-105
Given by Mrs E Ash, Killyleagh.

Uniform, Home Guard, comprising greatcoat, tunic, trousers, tie, two stripes (1 missing), gas mask in canvas bag and two caps.
These belonged to the donor's father, James W Clements of Downpatrick. You can see him in the photograph of Downpatrick Home Guard (Platoon 12). The Ulster Home Guard was formed in 1941, taking over from the Local Defence Volunteers, who were administered by the constabulary. The LDV had been set up in 1940 and members were armed but did not wear a

Home Guard, 2nd Down Battalion, Platoon 12. Mr Eric Malone can be seen in the second row from the back, third from the left, and Jim Clements is in the second row from the front, fifth from the right.

recognised uniform. This meant that they were not recognized combatants, according to the Geneva Convention, and could be shot if captured by the enemy. The Home Guard was administered and trained by the army from Lisburn. They were disbanded in 1944.
DCM 2004-274 to 281
Given by Mr David Clements, Downpatrick.

Seven fabric badges worn from the above uniform. Three are 'Ulster Home Guard', one 'Down', one with a crown, and two small square badges.
DCM 1998-129/1-7
Given by Mrs H Wood, Clwyd, North Wales.

Leather Anklets. They belonged to Mr Albert McCammon of Dundrum, who was in the Home Guard.
DCM 2004-287
Given by Mrs M I Maguire, Dundrum.

Uniform jacket, Auxiliary Territorial Service uniform, worn by the donor, who was a
Junior Commander in the ATS. Duties in the ATS varied from driving to gunnery.
DCM 2004-285
Given by Miss C M Wallace, Myra Castle, Walshestown, Strangford.

'Sam Browne' belt, worn by the donor who was a 2nd Lieutenant in the ATS at Ballykinlar Camp in 1939 under Junior Commander Miss Wallace.
DCM 1996-181
Given by Mrs M Torrens-Spence, Downpatrick.

Cap, American Officer's.
DCM 2003-132
Given by Mr S G McCracken, Castlewellan.

Pair of puttees, American Army issue.
DCM 1997-326
Given by Mr Joe Bingham, Newcastle (Patsy Mullen Collection).

Pair of black rayon stockings, part of WRN'S (Wrens) uniform.
DCM 1994-485
Given by Miss Lydia de Burgh, Clough.

Helmet, Street Fire Guard. This was issued to the Civil Defence Post 403, Orby Drive, Castlereagh Road, Belfast.
DCM 2004-291
Given by Mr James Rountree, Ballygowan.

Helmet, 'FAP' (First Aid Post).
DCM 1986-478
Given by Mr Tommy Hanna and Mr Kieran Feenan, Downpatrick.

Two civilian gas masks, in card boxes. One with name and address inside box 'J Rogers (Mr) Strangford Rd, Ardglass'.
Everyone feared gas attacks but these never happened, fortunately, since this kind of mask would have offered little protection against mustard and chlorine gas and none against nerve gases.
DCM 1986-498, 1997-324
Given by Mrs R Elliott, Bright, Killough and Mr John Murphy, Legananny (Patsy Mullen Collection).

Gas mask or 'helmet', for a baby.
DCM 1985-89
Given by Mr Desmond Maguire, Belfast.

Service gas mask in canvas bag (bag stamped '1941' inside), tin hat and stirrup pump. These were standard issue to those involved in Civil Defence. These items came from the home of the donor's mother-in-law, in Bangor.
DCM 2004-288 to 290
Given by Mr A Clough, Bangor.

Gas mask, stamped 'February' and 'March 1940', in canvas bag with drawstring closure.
DCM 2002-13/1&2
Given by Mrs M Thornton, Strangford.

Badges and buttons
Badge, metal, RAF. 3.7 x 4.1 cm.
DCM 1994-378
Badge, metal, Royal Corps of Signals.
2.9 x 4.9 cm.
DCM 1986-88/1
Badge, green and red enamelled metal, Ulster Home Guard. 2.1 x 2.4 cm.

Identity card.

The Home Guard items belonged to the donor, who, along with other members of his family, is in the photograph of Downpatrick Home Guard (Platoon 12).

DCM 1986-88/3, 1986-184

Badge, enamelled metal, Ulster War Savings. 2.6 x 2.5 cm.

Two certificates, Ulster War Savings, National Defence Issue.

Everyone was encouraged to save money for the war effort.

DCM 1986-128,1986-183

Given by Mr Eric V Malone, Ardglass.

DCM 1994-378

Given by Mr Eric V Malone, Ardglass.

Button, metal, with miniature compass inside. These were issued to RAF officers, to be used if they were shot down in enemy territory. 1.5 cm diam.

DCM 1994-411

Given by Mr J McCord, Ardglass.

Badge, metal, 'Spitfire Fund', issued to raise money to buy aeroplanes. 3.2 x 2.5 cm.

DCM 1994-363

Given by Mrs Joan Meneely, Newcastle.

Three buttons, metal, Royal Navy Officer. 2 cm diam.

DCM 1996-221

Given by Mrs Edith Ash, Killyleagh.

Nine buttons, metal, Royal Navy Volunteers. 2.3 cm diam.

DCM 1995-158

Given by Mr and Mrs A Johnston, Strangford.

Badge, metal, Royal Army Medical Corps. 3.4 x 4.5 cm

DCM 1994-221

Given by Captain and Mrs N Brownlee, Strangford.

Badge, metal, Royal Artillery. 6.6 x 5.1 cm.

DCM 1986-73

Given by Mr Desmond Fitzpatrick, Downpatrick.

Fabric insignia badge for a sergeant major in the Royal Artillery.

DCM 1996-123

Given by Professor R Buchanan, Strangford.

Fabric badge, Royal Observer Corps.

DCM 1996-44

Give by Mr Patrick McKay, Dundrum.

Ten buttons, white metal, 'CD' (Civil Defence). Eight are 2.2 cm diam; two are 1. 7 cm diam.

DCM 1995-102

Given by Mrs Joan Meneely, Newcastle.

Four fabric badges:

4CDY

'Belfast'

'Warden'

'10' (Incident Officer, Hampstead pattern badge, as worn in London Region).

DCM 2000-135 to 138

Four metal badges:

'ARP' (Air Raid Precautions), red and blue enamelled metal. 1.5 x 1.8 cm.

'ARP', silver, pin fastening, 2.5 x 3.7 ems.

Two 'ARP', cap badges, white metal. 2.5 x 3.7 cm.

The silver ARP badge is a type made at the beginning of the war and worn by Mrs McCord. The ARP was set up in 1938 but in 1941 was absorbed into the Civil Defence.

Although then administered by Civil Defence, the ARP still acted fairly independently.

DCM 2000-139, 1994-369, 2000-14 1/1 and 2

Given by Mr J and Mrs M McCord, Ardglass.

Badge, 'ARP', white metal, pin fastening. 2.5 x 3.7 cm.

DCM 1998-116

Given by Mr Noel Hogg, Newtownards.

Button, metal, 'ARP'. 2.1 cm diam.

DCM 1992-12

Given by Mrs A V Sterritt, Downpatrick.

Badge, enamelled white metal, 'The Sandes Soldiers and Airmens Homes. Est 1861'. 3 cm diam.[5]

DCM 1993-272

Given by Mrs E Montgomery, Belfast.

Five badges issued during the Second World War: Red enamelled white metal MWS Civil Defence (Women's Voluntary Service). 2.1 x 2.9 cm.
Red and green enamelled metal, Women's Land Army. 2.5 x 3.5 cm.
Blue and red enamelled metal, Civil Defence Corps. 1.8 x 2.5 cm.
White metal, 'For Loyal Service'. 2.4 cm diam.
Green and blue enamelled metal, Civil Defence (Irish Republic). 1.9 cm diam.
DCM 1996-60 to 63 and 65
Given by Mr D Patterson, Carryduff

Identity tag, white metal, American. 2.7 cm diam.
Three American Air Force badges, metal. 6 x 3.1 cm; 3.4 x 1.9; 3.3 x 2.9 cms.
Watch (strap missing), type bought by members of the Armed Services for six shillings. Badge, Herts Agricultural Executive Committee Women's Emergency Land Corp, yellow enamelled metal. 4.4 cms diam.
Three Royal Navy officer's buttons, metal.
DCM 1996-110, 112/1-3, 113, 118, 121
Given by Mrs E Ash, Killyleagh.

Button and badge, metal, American Army, First Armored Division. Badge 3.9 cm diam; button 2.1 cm diam. The Americans arrived in County Down in 1942 and had bases at Ballywillwill, Castlewellan, Mount Panther, Mourne Park, Newcastle and Tollymore.
American army circular fabric shoulder (flash) badge. This belonged to Joseph Gordon, Company B, 818th Tank Destroyers.
Fabric arm badge, rectangular, British Army, Royal Observer Corp. They were in this area of County Down in 1943.
American army issue leather wallet.
DCM 1994-361, 362, 1996-43 to 45
Given by Mr Patrick McKay, Dundrum.

Weapons, ammunition and tools
Two implements for scooping up incendiary devices, purchased by the donor's family after this kind of bomb landed near their house.
DCM 2004-292, 293
Given by Professor Ronald Buchanan, Strangford.

.303 calibre cartridge case, standard British Army rifle and light machine gun ammunition, found in the Mournes, where many of the troops did their training. DCM 1993-434
Given by Mr D Finney, Downpatrick.

After the war many people started new lives. This photograph, by Pat Hudson, shows a farewell dinner in the Royal Hotel, Kilkeel, for GI brides and their friends, mid 1940s. Second and third from the left are ? Cole and ? Donnan. Second and third from the right are Laura Rossi and Ellie Donnan.

Bayonet in scabbard, of a type used by the American Army, 1942. It belonged to the donor's brother, Captain Ralph Parkinson-Cumine MC.[6]
DCM 1993-313
Given by Miss Cecily D Parkinson-Cumine, Killough.

Army radio set, 19/22 principal AFV (armoured fighting vehicle) with instructions. Instructions dated 1942. This was designed and made in the United Kingdom and so successful that it was used by all Allied Forces. When the Americans entered the war, their radio sets, which had not been battle tested, proved to be very unreliable so they applied to the British Army to use this model. The donor bought this set after the war.
DCM 2004-336
Given by Mr J McRobert, Crossgar.

Parachute, partly re-made.
DCM 2003-73
Given by Mrs M Donnelly, Clough.

Ration Pack. This type of pack was given to British soldiers going into action. It consisted of a few tea and sugar bags, one oatmeal biscuit, one tin of steak and onion casserole, one packet of mock turtle soup and a packet of biscuits.
DCM 1997-327
Given by Mr P McCullough, Newcastle (Patsy Mullen Collection).

Pick and shovel, issued to British soldiers, for digging trenches.
DCM 1997-330 and 1997-331

Cutting tool, used by soldiers in Burma for cutting their way through the undergrowth.
DCM 1997-332
Patsy Mullen Collection.

Stirrup pump.
DCM 2004-267
Given by Mr F B McKeown, Ballygowan.

Cigarette lighter, bottom part made from rifle oil bottle, top from cartridge case and piece in top from bicycle (valve cover). This was made at Shorts Aircraft Factory. DCM 1998-159
Given by Mr J McRobert, Rademon, Crossgar.

Torch, made by Ever Ready in the 1940s for use in the Blackout. It could be clipped on to a belt to give a dim light around the feet.
DCM 1997-194
Given by Mr Richard Crory, Newcastle (Patsy Mullen Collection).

Generator used by the American Army based at Finnebrogue during the Second World War.
DCM 1998-53
Given by Mr Raymond Kelly, Dundrum.

Medals and memorials
Many men served in both World Wars. Some medals have therefore already been included in our article about the First World War, also in this issue of *Down Survey*.

Two Defence Medals, awarded to the donors for their work in Civil Defence. This type of medal was issued to Military and Home Guard, Ulster Special Constabulary, Air Raid Wardens, First Aid and Ambulance Services, Women's Voluntary Services and firemen and nurses.
DCM 1995-84, 1995-87
Given by Mrs Joan Meneely, Newcastle and Mr H A Porter, Dillon House, Downpatrick.

Two wall plaques, cream plastic, each 58.5 x 35.3 cm:
'Per Ardua ad Astra. War Savings campaign 1943. Presented by the Air Ministry in recognition of successful achievement in Wings for Victory Week'.
'For Freedom. War Savings Campaign 1944. Presented by the War Office in recognition of successful achievement in Salute the Soldier Week'.
DCM 1985-81/1 and 2
From the former Newcastle Urban District Council

Victory bell, white metal, with images of Churchill, Roosevelt and Stalin. 15.5 cm high, 11.5 cm diam.
DCM 2004-318
Given by Rev Dr W D Baillie, Saintfield.

Image from 'War Savings Campaign' plaque.

Books, newspapers, posters and other documents

Booklet, *Elementary Battle Drill for the Ulster Home Guard, No 1*, 1943.
DCM 2001-176
Given by Mr A Thompson, Newtownbreda.

Booklet, *Fighting Forces Handbook* by Arthur H Holmes.
Book, News in German by D H Stott, 1942.
DCM 2002-102, 2001-186
Given by Mr F Rankin, Belfast.

Book, *Basic Training in Air Raid Precautions*, 1940. This belonged to the donor's mother, Margaret, who was in the ARP.
DCM 2004-295
Given by Mr Eric V Malone, Downpatrick.

Booklet, *Make Do and Mend*, 1943. All materials had to be made to last as long as possible.
DCM 1996-209
Given by Mrs H Gregory, Belfast.

Four wartime cookery books:
Cookery in War Time, The Association of Teachers of Domestic Subjects, 1939.
Stork Wartime Cookery Book by Susan Croft, 1940.
A Kitchen goes to War, 1941.
Thrift Cookery Book, published by the Larkhill-Dalserf Branch of the WWS for Civil Defence, Scotland, 1941.
DCM 2000-3, 2000-21 and 22, 2004-102
Given by Mrs Marianne Brannigan, Rosconor, Downpatrick, Miss C M Wallace, Myra Castle, Strangford, and Mrs J Maxwell, Killyleagh.

Wartime Economy Recipes, recipes and information sheet. Recipes originally given on 'Gert and Daisy's' radio programme.
DCM 1998-143
Given by Mrs Anne McComb, Newcastle.

Newspapers: during the war, paper was in short supply and information was itself censored. *The Times*, 8 September 1939. Britain and France had declared war on Germany on 3 September.
DCM 2004-315
Anonymous donation

Booklet, *Make Do and Mend.*

The Down Recorder, 11 September 1943.
DCM 1989-11/1
Given by Mr E Moore, Lisburn.

Belfast Telegraph, 6 June 1944, headlines 'Invasion'.
DCM 2004-314

Two wartime magazines *The Eighth Army*, The Army at War series, 1944 and *Parade*, European Victory Number, 1945.
DCM 2004-316,1986-276

Punch on the Home Front, undated.
DCM 1996-187
Given by Mr Eric V Malone, Ardglass.

The Northern Whig, 3 July 1945.
2002-423
Given by Ms Marion Allen, Belfast.

The Times, 14 August 1945. Japan surrendered the following day. DCM 1994-498
Given by Mr Eric Napier, Comber.

Printed card, dated 8 June 1946. Victory message from George VI to school children. *Radio Times* magazine 10th May 1945 'Victory programmes'.
Belfast Telegraph, 6 June 1944 'Allies land in Northern France'.
Northern Whig, 8 May 1945 'Victory'
DCM 2000-104/6, 8, 9
Given by Mr R Forsythe, Killyleagh.

Daily Mail, 4 September 1939, Outbreak of War.
Northern Whig, 8 June 1944, Nomandy landing.
Sunday Express, 6 May 1945, German surrender.
The Times, 16 August 1945, Japanese surrender.
A short guide to Great Britain, published by War and Navy Departments, Washington DC, 1943. This was intended to help American troops based in the United Kingdom to understand the British way of life.
DCM 1002 2002-59 to 62, 2004-319
Given by Mr J Potter, Strangford.

Picture Post magazine Christmas Number, 27 December 1941. DCM 1996-126
Given by Dr R H Buchanan, Strangford.

Series of 12 posters issued during the war:
Careless talk costs lives (x 8), each 31 x 20 cm.
One aircraft now is worth two next year (x 2), each 37 x 24 cm.
One bomber now is worth two next year (x 2), each 37 x 24 cm.
DCM 1994-412 to 414
Poster, *Sleep to gather strength for the morning* (ARP).
DCM 2000-129
Five certificates awarded to James McCord:
By the Selection and Hanging Committee of Northern Ireland Civil Defence Exhibition of Arts and Crafts, 1943.
From St John Ambulance Brigade, Air Raid Precautions, 1938.
From Belfast Civil Defence Authority, Incident Officer's course, 1943.
Performance of Civil Defence Duties, 1941.
Card, 'Warden's Authority', issued by City and County Borough of Belfast certifying that James McCord was appointed Air Raid Warden, 1939.
DCM 2000-131 to 134
Given by Mr and Mrs J McCord, Ardglass.

Document, printed notice, *If the Invader comes*.
DCM 1009 2002-142
Given by Mr W Hanna, Crossgar.

Naval Pay and Identity Book, in the donor's name, 1942. DCM 1994-487
Given by Miss Lydia de Burgh, Clough, Downpatrick.

Christmas card, dated 1944, sent to his parents and sisters by the donor's uncle Eric, who was in the Royal Navy during the war. A photograph of the ship on which he served, HMS *Quality*, is inside the card.
Postcard, 'There will be a day of reckoning'. Bamforth card.
Postcard, 'Love to my Jolly Sailor Boy', Bamforth card.
DCM 1994-59, 2000-79, 2004-294
Given by Ms M Lesley Simpson, Balloo, Killinchy.

Christmas card, dated 1945.
DCM 2004-320
Anonymous donation.

Five Air Raid Wardens' Registers. These were issued to wardens and first aid points in Downpatrick, Downpatrick Rural Districts, Kilkeel, Kilkeel Rural and Newcastle. They were used to list the equipment held at the posts.
DCM 1994-327-327/1-5
From the archive of the former Newcastle Urban District Council.

Three ARP Documents:
Express Report book
Recruitment leaflet for Cyclist Despatch Corps
Civilian Duty respirator record card.
DCM 1996-201, 212, 213
Given by Mr G Curran, Belfast.

Message Forms, for reporting incidents such as fires in the Downpatrick area, 1942–1944.
DCM 2004-296
From the archive of the former Newcastle Urban District Council.

Application for a Travel Voucher. Travel was restricted during the war.
DCM 1994-516
Given by Mr and Mrs Douglas, Bryansford.

Ration book for food, 1944–45; clothing, 1945–46. Food rationing was first introduced at the beginning of the war, followed by clothes rationing and a utility scheme restricting the use of raw materials for clothes, furniture and toys in 1941. Food rationed ranged from meat and butter to canned fruit and breakfast cereal. Other rationed items included soap, razor blades and petrol. Shortage of petrol meant that it was difficult for people to travel, unless they provided essential services, for example, a doctor. Rationing continued into the 1950s.
DCM 1996-48 and 49
Given by Mr S Seed, Strangford.

Five National Registration identity cards. During wartime it was important to be able to establish the identity of people.
Card in the name of William Toman, Tievenadarragh, Clough, 1943.
Card in the name of Margaret McCord, Belfast, 1944.

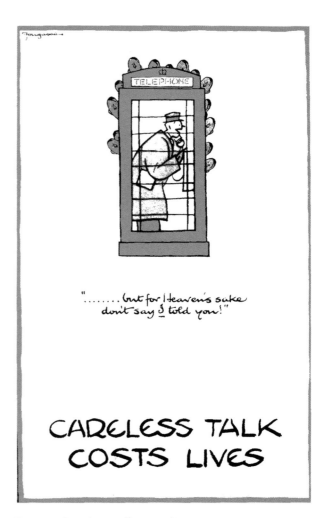

" . . . . but for Heaven's sake don't say I told you!"

CARELESS TALK COSTS LIVES

Poster, *Careless talk costs lives.*

Three cards in the names of Sydney M Gill, 1943, Doreen Gill, 1943 and Sydney Gill, 1942, all of Ballycruttle Downpatrick.
DCM 1996-90, 1995 -124, 1997-747 to 749
Given by Mr Patsy Toman, Tannaghmore, Loughinisland, Mr and Mrs J McCord, Ardglass and Mr T Lascelles, Downpatrick.

Instructions to stationmasters ... of Explosives ..., 1943.
Information sheet, Belfast and County Down Railway, Emergency Surcharges, 1940. DB445
DCM 1997-56 and 57
Given by the Downpatrick and Ardglass Railway Society.

Censor certificate, 1942, relating to the sending of parcels during the war. DCM 1997-674
Given by Mr F Rankin, Belfast.

Document, receipt for War Damage Contribution, dated 1942. DCM 1997-699
Given by Mr P J Lynch, Carryduff

Documents relating to service in the Armed Forces (ATS) by Miss Wallace of Myra Castle:
Letter from the War Office, 1943.
Letter about the age limit for officers in the ATS, 1945.
Two notes about promotion, 1945.
Two forms, one relating to re-instatement in civil employment (not completed), one an application for supplementary clothing coupons, 1944.
DCM 1999-89 to 93
Given by Mr D Good, Downpatrick.

Medical Hints incorporating Air Raid Precautions, Chorley District Nursing Association 1938.
DCM 2000-186
Given by Mr J Irvine, on behalf of the Downpatrick Property Trust.

Twelve programmes, for the Grand Cinema, Downpatrick, January to December 1941. It is interesting to see what films were being shown during the war. Charlie Chaplin's *The Great Dictator* was very popular in 1941.
DCM 1999-345 to 356
Given by Mr Lynn Corry, Raholp, Downpatrick.

Household and other objects
Nightdress, made from parachute silk. Silk was a real luxury and many young women managed to make their underwear from this source!
DCM 1994-484
Given by Miss Lydia de Burgh, Drumcaw, Seaforde.

Tin of dried eggs, 5 ounces, 12 eggs. Imported from the USA. 11.2 cm high, 7.5 cm diam.
DCM 2004-298
Given Mrs Mary Clint, Downpatrick.

Tin can sealer. This American-made gadget was used by Newcastle Women's Institute during the war.
DCM 1993-598
Given by Mrs Mary Imrie, Newcastle.

Glass sweet jar. The price of all items was strictly controlled but there was an extra ration of sweets at Christmas!
DCM 1994-84
Given by Mrs Ann Wright, Belfast.

Cooking vessel, in three parts, cast iron and aluminium, 'Dutch Oven'. This was used for cooking economically on a gas ring.
DCM 1994-85
Given by Mrs Ann Wright, Belfast.

Black metal box marked 'ARP'. Contains 5 enamel cups and saucers, white with blue trim; rectangular metal box; round metal box, sub divided and marked 'tea' and 'sugar'; expanding metal flask; oval-shaped wire mesh tea strainer. The box and its contents belonged to the donor's mother, Sylvia.
DCM 1994-261 to 266
Given by Mr A J Green, Raholp, Downpatrick.

Blackout curtain, double thickness of black linen union, 11 brass curtain rings attached. 1.30 m long x 92 cms wide.
The blackout regulations were introduced on 1 September 1939 and remained in force until 17 September 1944. You could be fined for showing light from a window during the night.
DCM 2004-317
Given by Mr and Mrs J Greer, Barnamaghery, Crossgar.

Contemporary board game, 'Bomber Command'. The winner was the first to reach 'Berlin', at the centre of the board.
DCM 1997-769
Given by Mr W Petticrew, Newcastle.

Wartime medical aids: Anti-gas eyeshields and 2 packets of shell dressings, one dated 1939, the other dated 1940.[7]
DCM 1994-515, 1994-492, 493
Given by Mr and Mrs G Douglas, Bryansford and Mr Les Jones, Ringawaddy, Downpatrick.

Works of art
Print of a painting by Mark Postlethwaite, '504 Squadron Down'. 65 x 97 cm.
DCM 1995-47
Purchase

Lesley Simpson is Keeper of Collections at Down County Museum. Noel Hogg has been a volunteer for 9 years.

Notes and references
1. See Mike King's Foreword in *Down Survey*, 2002.
2. You can read more about Lydia's experiences in *Lydia's Story* by Lydia de Burgh, 1991.
3. See 'Evacuees Stage Concert' by Mary E Croskery in *Lecale Miscellany* 3, 1985 and 'The Gibraltarians in County Down' by Mary E Croskery in *Lecale Miscellany* 12, 1994.
4. Captain Torrens-Spence (1914–2001) was awarded the DSO for his part in an attack on the Italian naval fleet at Taranto, southern Italy, in 1940. For his outstanding leadership and courage during other operations in the Mediterranean he was awarded the DSC and in recognition of his service to Greece, the Greek DFC. For more details see 'The passing of a hero' by Raymond Burrowes in *Ulster Air Mail*, March 2002.
5. The Sandes home at Ballykinlar is illustrated in 'Volunteers at the World's End' by Philip Orr, in *Down Survey*, 2002.
6. See also Swords and Pikes by Noel Hogg in Down Survey 1999.
7. See also 'From the Cradle to the Grave' by Madeleine McAllister and Lesley Simpson in *Down Survey*, 1999.

Acknowledgements
We would like to thank Tom Wylie, formerly Assistant Keeper, Department of History, Ulster Museum, for his assistance with this catalogue.

Eleanor Blair, née Love, with her two daughters, looking at a photograph in our 'Down in the War' exhibition. Eleanor is the child in the photograph while the lady in the spotted dress is Mary Love, who still lives in English Street, Downpatrick. This photograph was sent to us for copying by a former member of the Royal Welsh Fusiliers who now lives in Wales. It shows some of them outside the Old Down County Gaol (now Down County Museum) in Downpatrick, where they were based about 1940. The gaol was used as a barracks during the Second World War as it had been during the Great War

GI Stories of 1942

In May 1942, the First Armored Division of the US army arrived in County Down and made Castlewellan Castle its Headquarters, under the command of Major General Orlando Ward. The First Armored Division sailed from New York on the *Queen Mary* on 10 May, and arrived in County Down, via Greenock and Belfast, a week later.

As a result of a very successful visit to Cleveland by Andrew Carlisle to meet veterans of the First Armored Division, a number of photographs of the GIs in County Down have come to light. Among them are photographs of soldiers of the 123rd Ordnance Battalion, who were based at Downpatrick Racecourse, The Old Gaol (now the Museum), Ballykinlar Camp and other locations. Some photographs show soldiers of the 81st Reconnaissance Battalion, based first at Dundrum and later Spa, and senior staff at the Division's Headquarters at Castlewellan Castle.

Other photographs remind us of the route taken by the Division, once it left County Down in late October 1942. Having sailed from Larne to Stranraer, and arriving in Crewe on 22 October, the 81st Reconnaissance Battalion set sail from Liverpool in the *Empress of Canada* on 9 December, arriving in Oran, Algeria on 23 December. The Division played a major part in the campaign in Tunisia, which resulted in the surrender of the Germans and Italians on 9 May 1943. The Division then joined the Italian campaign, the 81st landing in Naples on the US *Liberty* on 24 October, and landing on the Anzio Beachhead on 28 January 1944. A determined German offensive kept the troops pinned down at

Horace Carratelli peeling potatoes at Ballykinlar Camp, 1942 (Courtesy of Horace Carratelli)

Horace Carratelli of the 123rd Ordnance Battalion at Ballykinlar Camp, wearing a 'soup-plate' helmet, before the new type of helmet was issued (Courtesy of Horace Carratelli)

Horace Carratelli, George Paneff, Nick Giacalone and mascot 'Ace' at Ballykinlar Camp, 1942 (Courtesy of Horace Carratelli)

Horace Carratelli's American National Red Cross Service Club Membership Card (Courtesy of Horace Carratelli)

Anzio, with the help of 'Anzio Annie', a German railway gun, which pounded the beachhead from inland. After the breakout and capture of Rome on 4 June, and a brief rest, the Division headed north. After wintering in the North Appenines, the 81st was involved in the final breakout into the Po Valley, which resulted in the execution of Mussolini on 28 April 1945 and the German surrender in Italy on 8 May, almost exactly three years after the Division's arrival in County Down.

The Museum is grateful to the veterans who have contributed their photographs, and to Andrew Carlisle for making contact and allowing us to use them in the *Down Survey*. The route taken by the 81st Battalion Company 'D' of the First Armored Division is well described by Laurel Anderson in his book *Return to Rapido* (Merriam Press, Bennington, Vermont) where many more details, including those events referred to above, will be found. The Museum would be pleased to hear of any other connections, photographs and artefacts which could help us tell the fascinating story of the GIs in County Down.

Photo of Thorl J Fitscher and Minnus L Montgomery of the 123rd Ordnance Battalion of the First Armored Division at the US camp at Downpatrick Race Track, 1942. The reverse reads: 'Taken outside the hut after we came in the other day. Plenty of air, plenty. I don't know why they took the time with the boards at the ends.' Later was added: 'Downpatrick, Ireland, the day we got rid of our soup-plate tin hats and got these, also new type combat rags, 1942' (Courtesy of Thorl Fitscher)

Horace Carratelli standing on top of the 'Leaning Tower' of Pisa. Part of his Division had to fire on the Tower to knock out a German outpost feeding information on US positions to artillery. A direct hit wiped out the position and several columns of the Tower, but fortunately did not adversely affect its 'lean' (Courtesy of Horace Carratelli)

'Anzio Annie', a 'German Railroad gun', captured in Rome, which had been used to fire on the invasion force at Anzio with great effect, and 'made the beachhead a headache' (Courtesy of Horace Carratelli)

Photograph of the First Armored Division Headquarters at Castlewellan Castle, September 1942. Major General Orlando Ward is pictured eighth from the left in the front row. The names of all those present are preserved in the Museum records

Montage of the above photograph of the First Armored Division Headquarters staff on a sketch of Castlewellan Castle, 1942